Not Alone

Also by Jenny Tomlin

Behind Closed Doors
Silent Sisters
(with Kim Challinor)

Jenny Tomlin

Not Alone

HODDER &
STOUGHTON

Complete identities, as well as names, have been changed in order
to protect the individuals whose stories are told in this book

Copyright © 2007 by Jenny Tomlin

First published in Great Britain in 2007 by Hodder & Stoughton
A division of Hodder Headline

The right of Jenny Tomlin to be identified as the Author of the Work has been
asserted by her in accordance with the Copyright, Designs and Patents Act 1988.

A Hodder & Stoughton Book

1

A CIP catalogue record for this title is available from the British Library

ISBN 978 0 340 92206 4

Typeset in Sabon by Hewer Text UK Ltd, Edinburgh
Printed and bound by Mackays of Chatham Ltd, Chatham, Kent

Hodder Headline's policy is to use papers that are natural, renewable
and recyclable products and made from wood grown in sustainable
forests. The logging and manufacturing processes are expected to
conform to the environmental regulations of the country of origin.

Hodder & Stoughton Ltd
A division of Hodder Headline
338 Euston Road
London NW1 3BH

This book is dedicated to the survivors whose stories are told here, and to the hundreds of thousands of others across the world. All of you are my heroes!

Acknowledgements

My thanks and love must again go to my wonderful family, for without their encouragement and love I would feel empty. Martine, as always, my inspiration, my strength and my friend. Words can never say enough about you.

Alan, you are always there, with endless cups of coffee and silent admiration for what I am trying to do – and you are always ready to make me laugh!

LJ, my rock and stability when I need to come down to earth.

Kim, constantly present quietly in the background, giving me the words I need.

Jaine, my manager and friend. You cheer me up and when I feel unequal to the task you inspire me with your words of wisdom.

To the lovely Caro Handley and her family for all the help in putting this book together and to the team at Hodder for their support and belief in what I have tried to do. A big thank-you to you all.

To all my loyal and loving friends – you know who you are – thank you. And finally to those who have shared a part of their lives with me: you need to know how truly amazing each one of you is. You are the foundations of this book and your stories make me humble, inspired and truly grateful.

Introduction

When I wrote my first two books I wasn't sure what the reaction from others – both those who knew me and those who didn't – would be. *Behind Closed Doors* was my account of the physical, sexual and emotional abuse I suffered as a child at the hands of my father. *Silent Sisters* (written with my sister Kim) was about the abusive relationship I got involved in as a girl of eighteen with the man who was to become the father of my daughter Martine. It took me nine long years to break free from him, and along the way I endured some truly horrific mental, physical and sexual abuse.

For me, writing the books was a turning point. For many years I had carried all the pain from those tormented years inside me. I did a good job of concealing it, leading a pretty normal life and bringing up my kids. But inside I ached with the burden of the memories that I could never shake off and the grief I felt at the loss of childhood years which should have been carefree and happy but which were instead filled with fear and dread.

Deciding to write down all that had happened, and

to go public with those memories, was a huge step. It's not easy to share publicly your deepest shame and hurt but for me it proved to be an incredibly healing and positive experience, and that was largely because of the response I got. I had decided to do it no matter what and had braced myself for disapproval or rejection. But in fact what happened was quite the opposite. Literally hundreds of people, both those I knew and those I didn't, got in touch to say how much the books had meant to them and how brave they thought I was to tell my story. I was deeply touched and felt delighted at this generous and welcoming response. My books had, it seemed, touched a deep chord with many people, folk who let me know how much they appreciated the honest telling of a painful but ultimately uplifting story.

Many of those who got in touch had their own stories to tell. I was astonished at the number of people who said 'It happened to me, too.' They also had hidden away their tales of suffering and abuse, often for many years. It seemed that I had opened up a route out of secrecy for others, many of whom wanted to tell me their stories. Some of them wanted to find their own way of going public too, in order to help lift the oppressive cloak of secrecy that keeps so much abuse hidden from view. They felt, as I do, that speaking out is one of the most powerful tools that survivors have for their own recovery, for helping others and for informing society at large about just how much abuse really does go on. Most of all, when you speak out you realise that you are not alone. The majority of people who are abused feel terribly isolated, as though they are the only sufferer in the world – I know I did. But in sharing the truth, you discover that many others have had similar experiences, and you are able to offer each other support, comfort, advice and even laughter.

It was when I was thinking about some of the accounts I had heard and how brave so many abuse survivors are that I decided to write this book. I wanted to tell the stories of some of the people I have met – both before my books were written and after – who suffered abuse and went on to recover and lead lives full of hope and achievement.

One thing I have learned is that abuse can happen to anyone, both men and women, from any background and at any age. It isn't about being a victim, attracting trouble or being in the wrong place. There was absolutely nothing that these survivors could have done to avoid what happened to them. Life throws the unexpected into our path all the time and although all who experience this trauma ask themselves 'Why me?' there is often simply no answer.

Abuse can take many forms, but in the majority of cases I have come across it is either wholly or at least partly sexual. For this reason, most of the personal accounts that I have included – though not all – are about sexual maltreatment. For me the most important aspect of all these stories is how the survivors coped. In talking to the people whose tales I have told I wanted to know what got them through, what gave them hope and what helped them to keep the abuse in perspective – as a part of their existence but not the whole of it. In other words, how did they stop what happened to them from taking over their lives?

The answers I got were fascinating and endlessly varied. For some, counselling helped. For others moving on meant putting what had happened behind them, in every way possible, and making a new start. Then there were those who relied on the support of friends and family, or who went on to help other survivors and so gave new meaning to their lives.

In many cases I could relate to these stories from my own experience. Because I suffered abuse as a child and as an adult too, I understood what many of the people I had spoken to had been through. But of course there were those who had tales completely different from my own. From all these people, both those I identified with and those whose experience I hadn't shared, I learned a huge amount. I am deeply grateful to all the people whose stories I have told here – and to the many more I have spoken to – for the insight, humour, courage and wisdom that they have shown and for the huge amount that they have taught me.

I
Rachel

Rachel and I have been friends for over twelve years and we know each other well. We've shared many intimate chats about life and love, so I thought I knew Rachel better than most. But one day she told me a story which made me realise that even when you grow close to someone some things can still be too painful to speak about.

Rachel's story touched a chord with me because it shows how vulnerable single parents can be. Like Rachel, I brought up my daughter alone for a number of years and I know only too well how much a mother in that situation longs for company, support and a man to love – and how easy it is to get it wrong.

As a single mum I was always very conscious that if I ever met a new man he had to be right for both of us – Martine as well as me. I was fiercely protective of her and was determined that I wouldn't let her meet anyone I dated until I was sure he was a good person, ready to cherish and be totally committed to us. But I know, too, how hard it can be to spot this knight in shining armour. Single mums have often been through the relationship wringer and come out the other side

asking themselves 'Who would want me?' So if someone appears keen and loving, it's easy to follow your
heart and not your head and think 'This is it.' It's all
too easy for a man who wants to take advantage of a
single mum to win her over – especially if he seems
willing to take on her child.

For Rachel all of these things were true. After a
painful end to her marriage she was vulnerable and
longed to be able to love and trust someone again.

It was while reading in *Silent Sisters* about the nine
years that I spent trying to escape from my violent
boyfriend Keith that she decided to tell me her own
story. Knowing that someone else has made the same
mistakes and fallen for an apparently kind and caring
man, only to learn that he was anything but, helps a
lot. At the time you think you're the only fool in the
world. Rachel did, and I know I did too.

I had met Keith when I was eighteen and still very
innocent. I thought he was wonderful and fell in love
very quickly. He was tall, dark, charming and very
attentive and he made me feel special. By the time he
began to be violent and possessive towards me I was
hooked and found it impossible to break off the
relationship. After every time he hurt or frightened
me he'd promise to change and would beg for forgiveness, and for a long time I believed him and
wanted to give him another chance.

Once our daughter Martine was born, I wanted
more than ever to make the relationship work. I hoped

and believed that fatherhood would change Keith and that he'd become more responsible and caring. But over time Keith only became worse. By the time Martine was a toddler he was terrorising and haunting me. Wherever I went he managed to find me, and he subjected me to cruel and violent sexual attacks and rapes which left me battered, crushed and fearful. Many times I ended up in hospital with horrific injuries including broken bones and cigarette burns.

It took me nine years to eventually free myself from Keith, with the help of a court order banning him from contacting me and Martine. But it took me a lot longer to feel safe and to really believe that we were rid of him. Because of what I went though I understand all too well what it's like to realise that the partner you love has another side to them, a side which is vicious and cruel. And I know how hard it can be to break free of someone like this. Just as you're determined to escape the monster, he switches back into the charming, loving man you fell for.

After reading my story Rachel must have known that I would understand hers.

Rachel began her tale in the mid-1980s when she had just returned from a spell living abroad.

She had married young and her husband had been posted to the Middle East to work in the oil business. Rachel had travelled with him and set up home for them and their small daughter, but things hadn't worked out. Rachel missed home and her friends and family: things became strained between her and her husband and eventually she decided to return to the UK. Devastated by the break-up of the marriage, she immersed herself in setting up home and starting a business. It was tough but, with her mother to look after her three-year-old daughter while she worked, Rachel managed.

She was a people person and loved organising, so it seemed a perfect notion when she decided to set up an events company. Knowing Rachel as I do, it was no surprise to me that, with her energy and determination, the business took off. Soon she was busy travelling and organising large corporate events as well as weddings and public service functions. From here Rachel takes up the story.

I was thrilled that my business was going so well. And when the local constabulary in my home area decided to put on a huge disco night for all their employees they came to me for help and I was delighted. I worked on it with a young policewoman called Paula, and over the months it took to set up the event we became very friendly. Paula would often call in to see me and we even went out socially together. This was great for me, as I'd had no social life since I had come back to the UK. I'd missed going out, but after my marriage ended my confidence took a dive and mostly I avoided social situations. So it was nice to have a girlfriend to go out for a drink and a chat with.

I began to feel I was getting my life back and everything seemed so good – I had a home, my mum to help me, a successful business and now a good friend too.

The night of the disco arrived and I was there early to ensure that everything would go without a hitch. As I checked on all the arrangements and made sure that everyone knew what they had to do, I noticed a young man staring at me intently. He approached and introduced himself as Simon, a detective inspector. I was too busy to take a lot of notice, but later in the evening he asked me to dance and I was really flattered – he was fun and easy to talk to. In fact we clicked immediately.

Simon was everything I liked in a man: tall and handsome, with the most amazing green eyes I had ever seen. I was bowled over that he was interested in me. After the break-up of my marriage I had convinced myself that I would be alone for a long time. I had just been getting on with work and caring for my daughter – I wasn't even thinking about finding a man. Funny how these things can happen when you least expect them.

Rightly or wrongly, Simon and I ended up in bed together on that first night. I surprised myself – it was totally out of character for me. If anything, I've always been a bit of a prude. But after so long without a man being interested in me I was swept away by his persuasive charm.

The following weeks were amazing. I was head over heels in love, and we spent as much time together as work would allow. My mother was so happy that I had found someone; she was brilliant and more than happy to have my daughter with her so that I could go out with Simon.

It didn't occur to me to doubt anything that Simon told me. So when he explained that he was an under-cover officer and that he preferred to keep things between us discreet and not to make our relationship public, I accepted it willingly, believing I was support-ing him in a difficult job.

Of course, I told Paula about my new man. I thought she'd know him and I was surprised when she said that she didn't. She warned me to be careful, but I laughed. I assumed that Paula didn't know about him because he worked undercover and that she was just being silly.

I thought long and hard about introducing Simon to my mother and my daughter, as I really wanted to be sure our relationship would last. But Simon convinced me that it would: he promised that we'd make a home together and said how much he longed to have a child. He always asked about my daughter and after a few weeks I felt secure enough with him to let him meet her.

For the meeting, we decided on an outing to the park for a picnic. I was excited and nervous at the same time. Everyone seemed to get on and things were going well until my daughter started to get upset. I didn't want her to go on the slide as it was too big for her and

I knew she would hurt herself. But, of course, she wanted to have a go. Suddenly, out of the blue, Simon grabbed her arm roughly and told her to be quiet. I was taken aback; it was the first time I had seen him angry. My mother looked at me and then took my daughter and led her away. There was an uneasy silence – I didn't know what to say. Simon apologised and said he'd just been over-keen to back me up, so in the end I didn't say anything. I told myself it was out of character for him and a one-off. But, looking back, I can see that his behaviour that day sowed a seed of doubt in my mind.

I decided that perhaps it had been a little too soon to introduce Simon to my family. A few days passed and Simon seemed as loving as ever, so I put the incident in the park to the back of my mind. And as the next weekend approached, Simon told me that he had something special planned.

That night, as I was getting ready, Paula called round. She told me that she could find no record of Simon being in the police force and she was worried. I argued with her, telling her that was to be expected. After all, how could he work undercover if everyone knew him? Paula told me he would still have been on record, even as an undercover officer. But I was sure there was a good explanation. I remember resting my hand on hers, thanking her for her concern and assuring her that everything was fine and that Simon was the one for me.

Of course, I should have listened to her doubts – and to my own – after what had happened in the park. But I was so happy to have found someone: I couldn't bear the thought of losing him, so I refused to allow myself to see that something might be wrong.

That night Simon had arranged for us to go with other friends of his to a club. I was thrilled to be going and was really looking forward to it. Simon picked me up and told me that I looked great. He introduced me to his friends and we headed for the club.

When we arrived it was packed and as we made our way through the crowds I noticed a girl looking at Simon. Later in the evening I went to the ladies' and the same girl was there.

She looked agitated and was biting her nails. She approached me and told me that she had been Simon's previous girlfriend and that he wasn't what he seemed. When I asked what she meant, she looked at me with tears in her eyes and told me to be careful. I remember thinking that she was behaving very strangely. She seemed frightened, and a chill ran down my neck. I decided to ask Simon about her after the night was over.

At the end of the evening we made our way home, a little the worse for wear but merry. I decided to make some vodka coffee while Simon put on some music. As I entered the front room with the coffee I saw that he had dimmed the lights and put on Spandau Ballet's song 'True'. He beckoned me over to him and as he put his arms around me he murmured that this was our song.

I leaned against his chest, but suddenly he grabbed my hair. 'What did the bitch say to you? Whatever she said, you had better not believe it.'

I was stunned. Simon let go of my hair, put his hands on my shoulders and smiled. I asked who he was talking about, laughing nervously as his grip on my shoulders tightened. 'Don't ever fuck with me, Rachel,' he said, pushing me down onto the sofa.

Even now I try to block out a lot of what happened that night. Simon raped me throughout the night, not caring how I felt and ignoring my pleas for him to stop. He was rough and violent and used force when I tried to stop him. I had no choice but to give in and by the time he was finished I felt hurt, ashamed and humiliated.

He left in the morning without saying a word, leaving me naked and bruised on the sofa. I was in shock, and perhaps that explained my behaviour. I realised that I must get myself ready for the day – and somehow I managed to block out everything that had happened the previous night. I can even remember singing to myself as I went into the bathroom. By mid-morning I was dressed and ready, and I'd cleared up the house. I started work, acting as if nothing had happened.

Paula called by and I still kept up the façade that all was well. I couldn't admit, even to myself, that I had been repeatedly raped throughout the night by a man who had seemed to be possessed. When Paula brought Simon into the conversation, I convinced her that all was well and that things were better than ever.

That evening, the doorbell went. As I opened the front door Simon walked past me into the house. He led me to the kitchen, sat me down on one of the chairs, sat himself down opposite and held both my hands. He started to cry and apologise for all that had happened. He told me his drink must have been spiked and that it had sent him crazy, and that someone was out to try and ruin his career. He said how sorry he was that he had hurt me. He was rambling and was desperate for forgiveness. I must have been completely insane, because I told him I loved him and all was forgiven.

But that dreadful night was far from a one-off incident. Over the next few months Simon raped me, viciously, many times. Each time he hurt me he would return the next morning with yet another explanation for his actions. To be honest, the reasons he gave were crazy, but he cried and apologised and time and time again I chose to forgive him.

I've asked myself many times why I did. Why didn't I walk away from Simon and get on with my life? All I know is that I was in complete denial. It was as though every time he attacked me I told myself it wasn't happening. I didn't want my dream man to be a monster – I wanted to hang on to the dream. And I didn't want to admit what a fool I'd been. The deeper in I got, the harder it became to face admitting that I'd got things so badly wrong. And there was another thing – I was afraid of him and I didn't want to face just how frightened I was. So I clung on to the idea that what he was doing wasn't so bad and somehow everything would turn out all right.

As time passed, my mother and my friends became increasingly worried about me. I lost a lot of weight, I was tired most of the time and my business was suffering. The one sane thing I did was to keep Simon and my daughter apart, and I'm glad that at least I had the sense to do that. When I saw Simon my little girl always stayed with my mum.

Paula continued trying to convince me that Simon was not in the police force, that he was not who he said he was, and that he was a conman who had probably done this sort of thing in the past, with other women. I brushed her off and even accused her of fancying my man. When I think how I treated her I feel ashamed – and so grateful that she stuck by me. And she did.

After coming round and finding me a nervous wreck one evening, Paula's frustration boiled over. She took me by the shoulders and shook me vigorously. Quite suddenly, I seemed to let all the pretence go and I came to my senses. I told her the truth, and after listening to me she said that I needed help to make sure that Simon didn't touch me again.

I had finally admitted to myself that Simon was not who he said he was. It was a relief, for me and for Paula, who had always known that something wasn't right. She took me to the police station, where I had to go over everything again. They promised to look for Simon and told me to phone them immediately if he came round. Then Paula took me back home, reassuring me that everything was going to be all right.

I was sure that I could handle things. But once Paula had gone I realised I wasn't as brave as I thought. I felt certain that Simon would somehow know I had reported him and would get me. My daughter was asleep in her room and I wished I had left her with my mum, where I knew she'd be safe. I sat rigid on the sofa, dreading the familiar knock on the door, and when it came, late that evening, I froze with fear. The telephone was staring at me, but I couldn't move to lift the receiver and call the police. Then all fell silent and I hoped he'd gone away. But suddenly I heard the back door forced open. Simon was inside the house. My thoughts went immediately to my daughter and panic set in.

As I sat trembling on the sofa, he entered the room. Without a word he moved to the stereo and put 'our song' on again. I looked at him and in that moment I realised that I had long ago stopped loving this man. Now I was simply terrified of him. His green eyes weren't beautiful, they were menacing. And his height, which had made me feel small and feminine, was intimidating. I realised that I was powerless against him.

I remember standing up and trying to run past him, only to be caught easily. He demanded that I undress. He watched as I reluctantly took my clothes off, savouring every minute. I prayed he would just have sex with me and leave. But when I was naked he grabbed my arm and led me to the kitchen.

Simon forced me to sit on a chair while he walked across to the cooker and turned on and lit all four gas rings. I was so frightened that I could feel urine starting to trickle down my legs as I watched him. He never said a word – he just smiled at me and then went to the cupboard and got a bottle of vodka. He opened the bottle and took a swig. Then he walked over to me and grabbed my neck, pushing my head forward. He poured the vodka over my hair, laughing as he did so. When I was soaked in alcohol he dragged me to the cooker. By this time I was screaming, begging him to stop, but it was as if he couldn't hear me.

As he held me by my hair over the burning gas jets the smell of vodka and singed hair filled my nostrils. The flames came closer and closer to my face and I passed out.

When I regained consciousness, seconds later, I was still being held by my hair over the cooker. The heat was unbearable, but I remember thanking God that at least I was still alive. A moment later there was a loud banging at the front door and I heard Paula's voice calling my name. She had come back to check on me. I remember being released and falling to the ground. As I did my cheek hit the side of the cooker. I felt no pain, but when I put my hand up to my face blood seeped through my fingers. Simon fled though the back door. I sat on the kitchen floor in a daze, blood on my hands, and all I could think of was that I was alive, my child was still safe, and Simon was gone. After a few minutes I pulled myself up and went to the door. I opened it and fell into Paula's arms. Shocked at my appearance, she wrapped me in a blanket and got a dressing for the wound on my face.

Paula wanted to go straight to the police but all I could think of was getting away. I knew I couldn't risk Simon finding me again. What if he evaded the police and came back to find me? I'd had a narrow escape, but next time he might well kill me – or, even worse, hurt my daughter. That night I took my daughter and went to my mother's. I had to tell her the truth, which was hard. She had worried about me for months, knowing that something wasn't right, but the truth was more shocking and frightening than she could have imagined. As always, though, she gave me her support.

The next day I went back home and packed as much as I could into the car before locking up the house and returning to collect my daughter from my mother's. We kissed my mother goodbye and by lunchtime we were on the road. I drove for three hours, to a town where I had an old friend. She put us up for a couple of nights while I found a small flat to rent.

Over the next few weeks I put my house up for sale and closed most of my business – I was terrified that Simon would track down my professional contacts and find my address. I kept a few clients – people Simon couldn't know about – and transferred them to the new business I was setting up in the town we had moved to.

Our new start wasn't easy. I had to leave everything and everyone I cared about. That was the price I paid for failing to see the early-warning signs about Simon and refusing to acknowledge the truth. Paula had tried to tell me, but I hadn't wanted to listen.

For months my daughter was unhappy and confused. She had lost her friends, as well as her daily contact with her gran, her nursery and her home. I did my best to comfort her, but at the same time I was a mess. The nightmare I had gone through with Simon had left me too thin, constantly anxious and without a shred of confidence. I felt unable to make new friends because I no longer trusted my own judgement. I became depressed and ended up going to the doctor and taking anti-depressants.

For a long time I still thought he would find me. Wherever I went I was constantly looking over my shoulder and would jump at the slightest noise. I had all kinds of security locks and chains fitted, I wouldn't go out after dark and when anyone came to the door I panicked.

My mother came to visit us and did her best to help. So did Paula, whose friendship still meant so much. She organised the sale of my house and when the money came though I was able to buy a new home.

But it took me a long time to feel anywhere near normal again, and the scars of what happened are still with me.

It was a heartbreaking story. But I couldn't help pressing Rachel a little further. Didn't she want to see this man punished? Didn't she want justice? If she'd gone to the police he would have been arrested and she would have been safe.

'Jenny,' she replied, 'you're my friend and you have known me a long time. I'm not a weak person, but back then I feared for my life and just wanted to run. I'm not proud of myself, but at that time all that mattered were me and my daughter: I just needed to get to safety and to put all memories of that man behind me.'

What happened to Simon? I asked. Did she ever hear of him again?

Rachel nodded. 'A few months later I had a call from Paula. It seemed that Simon had moved on to another victim, but this time he had been arrested on serious assault charges and the girl had agreed to give evidence. I felt a complete coward, but was relieved that someone out there had been stronger than me. When I heard later that he had gone to prison I felt huge relief, and I think that's when I started to put the pieces of my life back together again.'

She had definitely succeeded. The Rachel I knew was no coward. She was bright, outgoing and in a happy relationship with Peter, her second husband. Her daughter was twenty-two, had a lovely boyfriend and was working as a beauty therapist in a spa in town.

I asked Rachel how had she managed to trust a man again, after such an awful experience. It was a problem that I had encountered when I had finally come to the end of my relationship with Keith. For some time I looked on men as the enemy. If a man did anything that perturbed me even slightly I wouldn't see him again, and I wondered whether Rachel felt the same.

Rachel thought for a moment. 'I felt exactly the same for a few months, but I knew I had to move on, for my daughter. I was all she had and she deserved more than a mother who was a nervous wreck too scared to go out of the house. So for her sake I pulled myself together, one step at a time.

'Once I knew that Simon was in prison it helped. After that I put all memories of him away in a locked mental box and threw away the key. I got my new business going and settled my daughter in a nice nursery, made a few new friends and even did a part-time course in photography. But even after all this I wasn't ready for a relationship.

'I met a few nice men, but deep down I was still

afraid and unable to trust anyone, so I refused to get involved with any of them. Then, when my daughter was seven – four years after Simon – Peter came along. He was patient and caring and never questioned me about my past. In time I did find the confidence to tell him all about Simon. Like most decent men, he was horrified.

'Peter's love and care, his tenderness and humour, helped rebuild my confidence and heal the wounds. My daughter adored him from the start and he loved her like a father. After three years together I agreed to marry him and it was the best thing I ever did.'

Rachel had discovered one of the most important things in life, that a good experience is one of the best ways to overcome the memory of a bad one. I'd discovered the same thing. After Keith I eventually met John McCutcheon, a really good and decent man who helped me and Martine to feel safe, normal and loved again. I'd told John all about Keith and, like Peter, he was horrified and determined to look after and protect us.

'I know just what you mean,' I told Rachel. 'Peter helped you rebuild your trust, in the same way that John helped me. But don't forget that it was you who found the courage to face life again, to get out there and live, and to find him.'

Rachel smiled, and we raised our glasses in a toast. To good men – and brave women.

2
Fran

I want to tell Fran's story because it is deeply unusual. When people talk about abuse they usually assume that it involves people of different genders and that a man has abused a woman or a young girl. In fact abuse can happen in many different situations, and same-sex abuse by men is not uncommon. What is rare is a woman abusing another woman and, as Fran's story illustrates so powerfully, when it does come to light it is somehow more shocking because we hear of it so infrequently.

Fran decided to speak out after reading my first book, *Behind Closed Doors*. The abuse I suffered in my childhood left me, like most victims, with a huge sense of shame. It's this sense of shame that so often stops victims from speaking out about what they've suffered. When I told the story, very publicly, of what had happened to me, the greatest gift to come from it, and one I least expected, was that I no longer felt ashamed. A huge burden was lifted from my shoulders and I have walked a little lighter ever since.

Fran was the same. She had never talked about what happened to her, because of her huge sense of shame.

But, like the other victims of abuse whom I have met and spoken to since my books came out, she felt that my speaking out somehow gave her the courage to speak too. And I was so glad that she did. Stories like Fran's, shocking as they are, need to be told. If we do not speak of the unspeakable, how can we ever change society for the better? If abuse is shut away, victims are never freed from their hurt and shame and abusers continue to get away with their crimes. So I am proud of Fran for telling me what happened to her, and for allowing me to tell her story.

I first met Fran many years ago when we worked together in a recruitment agency. I was just eighteen and was thrilled when I got the job as her personal assistant.

From the beginning I really admired Fran. She was a few years older than me and very pretty, with beautiful long dark hair and olive skin. She had dark brown eyes and a warm smile and was bubbly and outgoing. She always seemed to be in control, and at work she handled people so well that it was no wonder she had been made a manager at such a young age. I was impressed and longed to be as confident as she was.

Each week, Fran and I would assign temporary office staff to local companies, to fill in for employees who were sick or on holiday. We were a very busy branch, and had little time for lunch breaks, but occasionally Fran and I would get away for an hour and go to a local department store. We'd search for new clothes or walk slowly around the perfume section, getting sprayed by the girls who were promoting different scents. We would test out new lipsticks and foundations and would often laugh and chat together.

Fran would often tell wonderful stories about her childhood. On the surface we had a lot in common. Both of us had two brothers and two sisters. But the similarity ended there. Fran had been brought up in a warm home, by loving parents. Her childhood was about as perfect as they come – she talked, her eyes shining, about birthday parties and cream cakes with her friends and brothers and sisters, or Christmas with lots of presents and celebrations and her unwavering belief in Santa Claus. She would describe how her dad cherished each one of the children, kissing and cuddling them in a way that made them feel safe and loved.

I suppose I was a little jealous of Fran and her unblemished childhood and I spoke very little about mine. How could I tell her about the filthy, dirty, cold flat we lived in, about the scruffy clothes we wore and how other kids called us the smelly Pontings because we were never washed? How could I tell her about lying in bed as a tiny girl, listening to Dad beating up Mum, or creeping through to the kitchen later to see her sitting at the table crying and trying to sellotape her glasses back together because he'd smashed them yet again?

It would have been hard for Fran to imagine a

childhood like mine, so full of fear and hurt and pain. How could I tell her that my father began sexually abusing me when I was four, and went on until I was a teenager? Or that he hit and humiliated us daily, terrorising all of us, including Mum, who was incapable of protecting her own children?

No, I could never have told Fran about all that. The shock and disbelief on her face would have been too much for me. And anyway, at that age I wanted to forget where I'd come from. Fran and the others I worked with were part of the new life that I was making for myself. I was happy that they knew nothing about me: it meant that I could move forward and be what I longed to be – a normal girl, like any other. Fran was all I aspired to be. To tell her how abused I had been as a child might have made her feel differently about me, and I didn't want that. So I said very little and when I had to I lied, pretending that my childhood had been normal and uneventful.

There was a time when Fran and I became really close and at one point I thought about confiding in her. But I was too scared, so I held back. Still, Fran was perceptive, and I always believed she did realise that something bad had happened to me in the past. But I never said anything, and neither did she.

At this time I was happily engaged to my first love, John Falconer. We'd met when I was fifteen and he was twenty-one and he'd been everything I'd dreamed of – kind, loving, intelligent and loyal. Fran, who had a nice boyfriend of her own, would often ask me if I felt too young to be engaged. Of course at the time I didn't, I was sure that the relationship would last for ever and that I was ready for marriage. But time would prove Fran right when, after a year at the agency, I decided that, after all, I was too young to settle down and wanted to see a bit of the world.

I parted from John and got a job in a holiday camp for the summer with my best friend, Sherri. I was sorry to say goodbye to Fran and my other friends at the agency, but excitement and adventure beckoned. So, with promises to stay in touch, I moved on.

Despite my good intentions I didn't keep in contact with Fran. Life took over and after my travels I found a new job. I had hoped that John Falconer would still be waiting for me, but he was angry that I had left and now there was no chance of us getting back together. His rejection left me heartbroken and weeks later, on the rebound, I met a new man. I fell for him completely and, at the age of nineteen, gave birth to my daughter Martine.

Many years later I moved to France to begin a new life with my husband Alan and my sister Kim. One day, a few years ago, I was at the airport, waiting to fly back to France after a visit to my family back in England. As I stood queuing to check in a woman came up to me.

'Hello, Jenny, it's me, Fran. Do you remember me?'

Of course I did. It had been almost thirty years since

we'd first met, but I was delighted to see her. And when she said she was booked on the same flight, on her way to visit friends who had also moved to France, I looked forward to spending the journey catching up with her.

Fran and I made our way to the departure lounge, where we waited to board our plane. Fran said how pleased she was about the success of my books and told me that she had read them both. She had been astonished, she said, to learn about the abuse I had suffered at the hands of my father and later from my partner. She told me how courageous I was to speak out and that it had made her think.

We boarded our plane and sat together, sipping coffee and chatting about our lives. Fran had never married, she told me, but had become a very successful businesswoman.

I was intrigued. 'Why didn't you marry?' I asked. 'I remember you had a boyfriend you were very close to. I always thought you'd marry him and have a family.'

'I thought that's what I'd do, too,' Fran said, slowly. 'But something happened that changed everything for me.'

She paused, the look on her face sad and thoughtful. 'I'd like to tell you the whole story,' she said. 'I've never spoken about it before, but perhaps now the time is right. Would you mind?'

I assured her that I would be happy to listen, wondering what could have happened to change the direction of her life so drastically. Had something gone wrong between her and her boyfriend?

As Fran told her story I listened quietly. I didn't interrupt her, knowing that once she'd begun she needed to get it all out. The tale Fran had to tell was bizarre, but I knew without a doubt that she was telling the truth. 'It was so long ago,' she began, 'but I remember it as if it was yesterday. Everything in my life was good then. I had a nice flat, a well-paid job at the agency and a lovely boyfriend. You remember how it was. My home life had been so happy and I feel guilty, now I know what happened to you, Jen, when I think of how I twittered on back then about my great family.'

Fran paused. I could see that this was difficult for her. She stared down at her hands as she fumbled with her napkin, and then she started to speak in a low voice. *What follows is Fran's story in her own words.*

I had a girlfriend called Amanda. We became instant pals on the day we started secondary school together and throughout our school years we were the very best of friends. After we left school I went into office recruitment as you know, and she went into nursing. Despite her shift work, we still managed to meet up and often had some very wild nights, drinking and dancing. It was so much fun – Amanda was the life and soul of every night out, and we always looked out for each other. Neither of us had a steady boyfriend so we spent a lot of time together.

When Amanda decided to move out of the nurses' accommodation at the hospital and needed a place to live, it seemed the perfect solution for her to move in with me. I had a little flat in Camden, with a spare bedroom, and she was really happy when I suggested that we could become flatmates.

From the start we got on really well. Living together could have put a strain on our friendship, but in fact it only made us closer. We shared all the household tasks – washing, shopping, cooking and cleaning – and we never argued. I was delighted because Amanda's rent helped with the bills and I had a good friend to come home and chat to at the end of the day.

A few months before Amanda moved in I had met John – the boyfriend you remember. We started going out together and before long we were in love. I thought he was the perfect man – kind, good-looking and very loving. So I was a little hurt and disappointed that Amanda didn't seem to take to him. When I first introduced them John made a real effort to be nice to Amanda, knowing that she was my best friend. But she didn't respond. Instead she told me that she didn't think he was right for me.

I was puzzled. John and I were really happy together, so why wouldn't Amanda be happy for me? She never really explained – all she would say was that he wasn't good enough for me.

I put it to the back of my mind, hoping that when Amanda met a boyfriend of her own she would understand how I felt about John. She never seemed to have a boyfriend, but I was sure that it was just a matter of time until she did. Meanwhile, after a few uncomfortable evenings, I gave up including Amanda when I was going out with John, and just saw the two of them separately. If John was coming round to the flat Amanda would disappear into her room, or would go out.

We carried on like this for several weeks. Then one evening I arrived home from work soaked through from a heavy downpour. Amanda was busy revising for her nursing exams and had already started preparing supper. I shouted to her that I would take a quick shower before dinner. I headed straight for the bathroom, dropped my wet clothes on the floor and got into a hot shower. I hadn't locked the door – we hardly ever did as there were only the two of us in the flat. We didn't normally walk in on one another, so I was a bit surprised to find Amanda standing there when I stepped out of the shower. 'Hi,' I said. 'What's up?'

For a minute Amanda said nothing, but the odd, intense look on her face made me feel uncomfortable. I was naked and soaking wet, so I reached for my towel. But she blocked my way.

Suddenly she began screaming at me. 'You fucking bitch, you selfish cow, I hate you and I hate him'.

I was shocked. What on earth could she mean? Her face was twisted with hatred, her teeth clenched as she spat angry words at me. 'I'm sick of you shoving your stupid boyfriend under my nose – can't you see he's just a pathetic fool?'

I suddenly felt very afraid. I had never seen her like this before. 'Amanda, calm down. What's got into you? You're behaving like a madwoman.'

'Yes, I am mad,' she said, 'and I've had enough. You belong to me, not him.' It was hard to take in what she was saying. How could I belong to her? But her meaning soon became all too clear.

How I got onto the bed in her room I don't re-member – she must have dragged me out of the bath-room. All I can remember is that my body was still wet and that I felt the cover on the bed sticking to my skin. Amanda was surprisingly strong and, despite my struggling, she had me pinned down. Her mouth was all over my face and her fingers were scratching at my body.

I was horrified. Was Amanda a lesbian? Why had I never known? She hadn't given me a single sign – or perhaps I had just missed the clues because it hadn't occurred to me.

Summoning all my strength, I pushed her off me and managed to get myself upright so that I was sitting on the bed. Beside me, Amanda's face was deep red with anger. I was feeling very disorientated so I didn't see the punch coming. But I certainly felt it – it was so powerful that it knocked me out. When I remember it I can still feel it right here, on my jaw.

I came round moments later to see Amanda, her face looming over mine, straddling me with her legs either side of me. To my horror she had strapped a large rubber penis around her hips. She pulled my legs apart and suddenly I felt the dreadful thing thrusting into me. It was cold and very hard and the pain was excruciating. The only sex I had ever experienced before this was with John and it had been warm, gentle and loving. What Amanda was doing to me was cruel, degrading and desperately painful.

My heart was pounding so fast and I could hear it thumping. This could not be happening to me. This was my friend. We had shared so much together – now suddenly all that was meaningless. I tried to reason with her, but it had no impact. Neither did my screams of fear and pain.

Amanda continued to thrust the object into me, harder and harder. As I sobbed she was touching herself sexually and writhing about. I tried to struggle but it was hopeless and in the end I just lay there until she had finished.

I don't remember what happened next – I only remember waking up in the early hours of the morning. The flat was silent, but I was terrified that Amanda was still there, waiting to attack me again. Slowly I got my painful, bleeding body off the bed, turned on the light, found my dressing gown and wrapped it around me.

I tiptoed around the flat, my heart pounding. But it soon became clear that Amanda had gone. Her bedroom door was open and all her clothes had been removed. In the kitchen the blackened remains of the lasagne that we'd been going to eat for supper were still in the oven.

Relief flooded through me. Once I was sure that she wasn't there I ran to the front door and locked it. Then I ran myself a bath and sat in it for an hour, trying to scrub every trace of her from my body – and with them the hideous memories, too. But of course I couldn't – what Amanda had done went through my mind over and over again. How could my friend, my best friend, have viciously raped me? The memory of the hatred in her face was as awful as the horrendous pain she inflicted.

For days I locked myself in the flat. Looking back I realise I must have sunk into a deep depression. Everything I did was robotic. I called in sick at work and when John rang I told him I had flu and needed to rest. I couldn't face the world: I just sat in the flat, trying to understand what had happened. It was clear that Amanda had been desperately jealous of John and had wanted me herself. But what had turned her into a psychopath who was capable of such a violent attack?

I couldn't even begin to understand her. She had been so angry – she must have bottled up her true feelings for years, until they came out in an explosion. I wondered whether she realised just how much damage she had done to me.

Logical or not, I felt ashamed that it had happened, as if it had been my fault. I couldn't bring myself to tell anyone. It would have been bad enough saying I'd been raped by a man, but a woman? I felt sure that few people would believe a woman had sexually attacked another woman. I can remember my dad phoning me soon after it happened and I just carried on the telephone conversation in the most bizarre way, laughing and chatting as if nothing had happened. As I replaced the receiver I began to sob uncontrollably.

As well as feeling the pain from the bruises on my face and body I knew that I was badly injured internally. I bled for days and going to the loo was agony. But I was too traumatised to see a doctor – it didn't even occur to me. I just stayed in the flat, endlessly cleaning and scrubbing to remove all traces of Amanda and to try to make myself feel better.

It's hard to remember how I got through those long dark days. At the time they seemed to go on for ever. I felt more dead than alive and I spent hours just lying in bed, staring at the wall. I felt cut off from the world, as though what had happened had made me different and set me apart from everyone else. I often wondered if I was falling apart and if life was worth living any more.

Then, a couple of weeks after the attack, I got up one day and noticed that the sun was shining. It was glorious weather outside and I suddenly wanted to feel the sun on my skin. I decided to walk to the newsagent's and buy a paper. It felt like a huge thing to do and I had to get up my courage. But I did it and no one stared at me or looked at me as if I was a victim.

After that, each day I grew a little stronger and a little more determined that what had happened wouldn't destroy me.

Eventually I went back to work. Everyone noticed that I was quieter than before, but I told them it was just because I had been unwell. I couldn't afford to lose my job, so I threw myself into work and was soon offered a promotion.

As for John, my relationship with him didn't stand a chance. He had no idea what had happened to me and I couldn't bring myself to tell him – I was so afraid that he'd reject me and think I was a fool if I did. I told him that Amanda had just decided to move out and that I didn't want another flatmate. But he couldn't understand why I had changed. I flinched whenever he touched me, I couldn't bear the thought of sex and I picked arguments with him all the time. Looking back I think this was partly because I wanted to keep a distance between us physically, and partly because I blamed him in some way for not looking after me and somehow preventing the attack. Of course this wasn't logical – he couldn't possibly have done anything to stop it – but I still felt angry with him. After a few weeks of being pushed away he gave up trying to reach me. We broke up and I felt relieved. All I wanted was to be alone, without anyone trying to touch me or come close.

I never heard from Amanda again and I tried to forget the whole horrible incident. I moved away from Camden, but I still had nightmares that were so bad I would wake sweating and in tears.

It was a year before I went to a doctor. I told him that I had been raped by a man some time before, and that I thought I had been injured. He was understanding and sympathetic and examined me gently. He confirmed that I had been badly injured – there was a lot of scar tissue internally – and he suggested that I should have some tests.

The results of the tests confirmed that I would never be able to have children.

I think that was my lowest point. I wept for weeks after I learned the awful truth. Amanda had destroyed my confidence, my relationship and now my chances of having a family.

How could I ever marry, knowing that I would never be able to give my husband children? Having had such a happy home life myself, I'd always wanted children, so I felt as though my world had ended.

It was another year before I went on a date – my first in the two years since I'd broken up with John. But the relationship had no chance because I refused to let the man get close to me. That became a pattern – I'd be alone for months, then finally I'd go out with someone, only to push them away within a few weeks or months.

I just couldn't face telling any man the truth – I was sure that they would reject me if I did.

Looking back I think that, deep down, I had made a decision to live my life alone. So I poured all my hopes and my energy into work, eventually starting my own agency and becoming very successful. I bought a nice home and made a good life for myself.

I've spent a lot of time alone, probably far more than I would have if it hadn't been for Amanda's attack on me. I think in some ways it changed who I was, made me much more reserved. But I was never a quitter and even after the devastating news about never being able to have children I was determined to make the best of what I had. And as the years have gone by the memories of what happened have faded and I've been able to find joy again in all kinds of things. That's important to me, because I really did love life before, and I didn't want to let Amanda take that away from me. I'm grateful for what I have. There's only one real sadness left, and that's that I haven't managed to make a good relationship with a man.

As Fran reached the end of her story she looked up at me. She sighed heavily and then switched on her memorable smile. 'I've managed to put what happened behind me,' she said. 'But strangely it's some of the trivial things that still remind me. Like the blackened lasagne we were to have for supper that night. I've never been able to eat lasagne since.'

I reached gently for Fran's hand and thanked her for telling me. 'How did you rebuild your life after living through something so terrible?' I asked her.

Fran thought for a few minutes. 'Well, at first I just wanted to be invisible. But later on something else kicked in. A determination not to be beaten. I was very loved as a child and because of that I grew up with high self-esteem – I felt good about myself and confident about life. Amanda nearly destroyed that, but it was deep within me, and bit by bit that self-love saw me through.

'I was very angry for a long time, angry with her and angry with myself for letting it happen. I would question myself time and time again, asking myself whether it had been my fault, whether I'd provoked it. But the conclusion I came to was always the same. It had been Amanda's fault, not mine. Accepting this was the biggest step forward of all, and once I did I was able to start to love myself again.

'It took a few years to come to terms with this and stop blaming myself. And in the meantime work became my therapy. I was good at my job and I did well and that also helped me to feel good again. My work took me all over the world and eventually the memories of Amanda and that night came to me less fiercely.

'Sometimes I could cope with the flashbacks and sometimes I couldn't. There were nights when I would wake up and the nightmare had returned, but over the years they became less frequent.

'I also felt that it might have helped if I'd been able to understand how Amanda felt, and what was really going on inside her head. Perhaps I might have forgiven her, but then again, perhaps not.'

Fran smiled. 'I'm glad I've told the story at last. I feel a weight has been lifted from me'. She opened her arms to me and we hugged.

I was left feeling inspired and humbled by Fran's incredible story. Although I had suffered abuse myself, both as a child and as an adult, what had happened to Fran shocked me to the core. I wondered how another woman could do such things, especially to someone whom she is supposed to love. It seems difficult to believe, though, that it *was* love that motivated Amanda – it sounded more like a jealous obsession.

What mattered ultimately was that Fran had come through it and had grown, from the experience, into the wise, warm woman I had met at the airport. When we reached our destination we said goodbye and promised to stay in touch by email. And this time we did, sending each other regular updates about our lives and plans. Last time she emailed me she was doing business in Japan but, more importantly, she had met a new man. The email was full of her love for him. She had told him everything and he had understood and had offered her his love and support.

She told me that at last she felt ready to give all the love she had to him. She said that it was as if a black cloud had disappeared: after all this time she no longer had to paint on a smile to face the world because she was smiling for real.

I was so happy for Fran. Finding the courage to tell her new man the truth had been a turning point. Now she is able to let go of the shame and finally enjoy the happiness she so richly deserves. And she's setting up home with her new man in the Lake District . . . go, girl!

3
Beth

Beth's is a story that I identified with very strongly, as I'm sure many other women will. She was abused by a trusted senior family member, someone who was supposed to love and care for her but who took advantage in the worst possible way.

A small child is so helpless, and so often has no one to turn to, and isn't believed even if they do try to tell what they are going through. In the days when Beth and I were abused – me by my father, Beth by her grandfather – this was especially true. Adults generally believed other adults, not children. So we were left to suffer, knowing that there was no way out.

Nowadays things are a little better. Children still suffer, but many adults are more aware that abuse goes on, and are more ready to listen to a child. And there are wonderful organisations that abused children can phone, in confidence, for help. How I wish they had existed when I was a small girl desperate to escape my father's cruel and horrific assaults and how glad I am that children now have a greater possibility of someone to turn to.

I've included Beth's story because I believe that if

people like Beth and I speak out about what has happened to us, then more people will become aware of how the unthinkable can actually be going on in their own homes. We need, every one of us, to be alert to the possibility of abuse and to the signals that an abused child will send out. If we shut our eyes and ears then we risk betraying children who are lonely, frightened and desperate.

Beth is a fairly recent friend. We met through a mutual acquaintance who invited us both over for a meal. I liked Beth straight away. In her early fifties, with the figure of a twenty-year-old and stylish grey hair, she had twinkling blue eyes that lit up her small round face.

After the dinner we agreed to meet again, and when we did we talked about everything under the sun before getting round to the subject of books. When she realised that I was the author of *Behind Closed Doors*, Beth gripped my arm tightly and said 'I read your book in a day and just couldn't put it down.' Beth went on to say that reading about how my father had sexually abused me from the age of five to eleven had brought back memories of her own childhood. She paused, unsure whether to go on, but when I asked her about what had happened to her the words came out in a torrent. It was as though she had been holding back for so long that, when at last she decided to talk, it was like a dam bursting. Here is Beth's story as she told it to me.

*　　*　　*

I grew up in the 1950s as the only child of well-off parents who gave me everything they could. My mother had a full-time job – which was unusual for a woman in those days – as matron at the local hospital. Dad was in the construction business and was often away, sometimes for weeks on end. When they were both working I was sent to my mother's parents' house, a few miles away from home. I went a couple of times every week, and sometimes spent the weekend with them.

I would go into their house through the back door that led into the kitchen and Nanny would always be there, with something delicious cooking on the stove and a fresh pot of tea on the table. Nanny spent a lot of her time cooking. In the 1950s a woman's place was in the kitchen, and despite her job my mother always found time to cook for me and my father, using the recipes that my grandmother had passed on to her.

My grandmother was a lovely round woman, with a big smile and a huge cuddle to match. When I arrived she would throw her arms around me before sitting me down for a glass of juice and a slice of home-made cake.

But it was very different with Grandad. He was a tall, slim man who had been very strict with my mother and was the same with me. He would often sit in front of the fire, reading the Bible and smoking his pipe. He'd make me recite verses from the Bible, insisting that I spoke God's word clearly and with passion. He made a big impact on me and I grew up fearing God, for as far as Grandad was concerned God's word was law and should always be obeyed, or there would be severe punishment.

On cold winter nights, with the fire roaring, Grandad would pull me onto his lap and squeeze me hard. I didn't enjoy his cuddles with me – they weren't soft and loving like Nanny's – but I was much too afraid to disobey him. I would look forward to bedtime, just to get off his lap.

In the winter of 1956 the weather was much worse than in previous years. A flu epidemic had broken out in our local area and my mother was busier than ever at the hospital. My father had been called away on business for three weeks and it was decided that I should go and stay with my grandparents for most of that time.

Nanny was thrilled to have me, and for the first few days things were wonderful. During the day I helped Nanny with her baking. Her bread and biscuits were delicious. In the evenings I would sit with her, sewing and making bead necklaces and bracelets. We also enjoyed jigsaw puzzles, especially the ones with pictures of exotic places. Then, just before bed, Nanny would make me a milky Ovaltine and then come up with me to tuck me in.

On the first night when my grandfather interfered with me Nanny had gone to visit a sick friend a few streets away. Grandad had told her not to worry about me, and that he would tuck me in that night. He did much more than that. I really can't bring myself to speak of what he did. I can only say that it hurt and that he told me God would send me to hell if I told anyone.

After he had gone I lay in the dark, frightened and hurting. I was just seven years old. Looking back, what I remember most is feeling so alone, knowing that I wasn't to tell anyone. I didn't know that what Grandad had done was wrong, but I knew it hurt and frightened me and that I didn't want it to happen again.

Later, after it had happened many more times, I realised that he shouldn't be doing these things to me. But at first I was uncertain and confused. It was the secrecy of it all that made me understand that these things shouldn't be happening. It was the way he made me swear on the Bible that I wouldn't tell anyone, especially Nanny or my parents. It was also the way he stared at me when Nanny or my mum was in the room, and that sickening smile he gave when he knew I wouldn't speak. He had a hold over me, and I felt helpless to do anything about it.

I began to ask my parents not to send me to my grandparents' house. I begged them to send me to stay with a friend instead. But they couldn't understand what I was making a fuss about. My mother would say 'But you love Nanny and Grandad, and they love you. I wouldn't want anyone else to look after you.' If only she had known. But of course she had no idea. I longed to tell her, but if she didn't listen to me when I said I didn't want to go why would she listen to me telling her that her own father was assaulting me?

Now, as an adult, I've wondered whether he had assaulted my mother in the same way. Perhaps he had and she was in denial. Or perhaps he hadn't and only assaulted me, later in his life. There are so many things I will never know.

When I was at my grandparents' house I tried everything I could to avoid being alone with my grandfather. If Nanny was going out shopping, or to see a friend, I'd beg to go with her. Sometimes she let me, and I'd be so relieved. But my grandfather would tell her that he enjoyed having a bit of time with me, so more often she left me with him.

I was nine when he first had full sexual intercourse with me and the rapes continued until I was twelve. I was not an early developer and, looking back, I wonder what might have happened if my periods had started earlier. The thought of it makes me feel ill. Luckily, the dreaded curse, as my Nanny used to call it, didn't happen until a few years after my grandfather's death.

Beth paused. I knew just how she felt. As a small girl I had been bewildered and frightened when my father began creeping into my room at night to abuse me. Although he never had intercourse with me he did just about everything else, forcing me to have oral sex with him and using his mouth and fingers on me. Like Beth, I didn't understand why he was doing it, but it took a while for me to realise that it was wrong. A small child doesn't know that abuse is wrong – how would they? I used to wonder if it was happening to other girls, though deep down I felt sure that it wasn't. By the time I understood how wrong it was I was powerless to stop my father. He was a big man and could force me to do whatever he wanted. My little sister Kim got the same treatment – we would try to help and protect each other, but often there was nothing we could do. Our father would humiliate and terrorise us, not only abusing us but beating us and letting us go hungry.

I asked Beth whether she ever tried to tell anyone. 'I came close,' she said. 'But I never managed to come out with it. I would hover around Nanny, trying to find the right words. Once she even asked me what was on my mind – she could see that I was distressed. But in the end I was too afraid to tell.'

I had wanted to tell someone too. Not my mother, who I believe knew of the assaults and turned a blind eye, grateful that when my father was molesting me or Kim he wasn't attacking her. The person I longed to tell was Auntie, the kind and loving aunt who rescued us from our parents as often as she was able. I think Auntie would have believed me, but she would also have felt that she had to confront my father, or report him. And he would have stopped us seeing her. That was the one thing I couldn't risk. The time we spent with Auntie, odd days or weekends and, in the holidays, even whole weeks, was so precious that I couldn't risk losing it. Without the sanity, cleanliness and comfort of Auntie's small flat and her plump embracing arms, our childhood would have been without hope.

I asked Beth how the abuse eventually stopped. In my own case my father gave up abusing me when I grew big enough to fight back and threaten him. I wasn't worth the trouble after that, and in any case there were my two younger sisters he could turn his attentions towards. But in Beth's case it ended with her grandfather's death.

'He became ill,' she said. 'It was when I had just celebrated my twelfth birthday and had been on my usual visit to Nanny and Grandad's house. I had stayed overnight, and once again Nanny had popped out to a friend's, leaving me with Grandad. I knew he would expect sexual intercourse and although I hated and dreaded it I just did it. There was no point in fighting him and I just wanted to get it over with as soon as possible. After each assault I felt a kind of relief, because I knew I wouldn't have to go through it again for another week or so.

'After Grandad climbed off me, he started to cough and wheeze. He was obviously in some discomfort, but I didn't care. Actually, I was pleased to see him suffering: I wanted something to happen to him so that he wouldn't be able to hurt me any more. Over the next few weeks the cough got worse and finally, after some persuasion from Nanny, he went to the doctor's. It was lung cancer.

'Within months Grandad was admitted to the hospital where my mother worked. We made regular visits to the hospital to see him, but most of the time he was heavily sedated and was asleep. I hated going to see him, but every time I saw him in the hospital bed I felt relieved that he was still there and couldn't come near me.

'Visits to Nanny's were now an absolute pleasure for me, and despite her concern for my grandfather, she seemed different – lighter and happier. She stopped being a slave to the kitchen and began going out more and seeing more of her friends.

'After just a few weeks we received the news that Grandad was dying. I remember getting in the car, wearing my best Sunday dress. It seemed appropriate, as this was the last time I would see him. Everyone had dressed up to say their goodbyes.

'As the family huddled around his bed I stood back. There were uncles and aunts, cousins and friends that I had barely met before, all wanting to be with Grandad before he died. My mother took my hand and led me to the side of the bed. 'Kiss Grandad goodbye, Beth,' she said. I stood there rigid, staring at his yellow skin and dry shrivelled mouth, and shook my head. I had never defied my mother before but I knew I would never kiss this man, even in his dying moments. I think my mother just assumed that I was in shock and was upset.

'When I was told that he was dead I felt relief. He was gone and would never touch me again. But I felt guilty too. He was my grandfather: I knew I shouldn't have wished him dead, and yet I'd wanted it so much that I'd prayed for him to die.

'It was a long time ago, but I have never forgotten, neither have I forgiven that man. He was my grandfather and should have been my protector, not my persecutor.'

I asked Beth if she would consider telling anyone else now that she had spoken to me.

'I would if I thought that it would help anyone else. I'm happy for my story to be told if it will encourage other children to speak out and adults to listen.'

Did she feel she had recovered? I wondered.

'Yes, in many ways I have,' she said. 'My grandfather's death was the key for me. It was so final. I knew that my abuser was gone and I would never have to see him or suffer at his hands again. It set me free.'

Although my father died years after the abuse he had inflicted on me I know the feeling of pure joy and relief that Beth experienced. In a strange way death is a form of justice being done.

As Beth explained, 'My grandfather is part of my

past, not my future.' She had been released and although the memories wouldn't disappear she knew she could move on. And she did. Beth led a full life, with marriage and children of her own.

And today? 'I have a wonderful second husband and a smashing life and I'll continue to enjoy my children and grandchildren, with pride.' Beth smiled.

'If there's one good thing that has come out of this, it's the care I've taken to make sure that my own children and grandchildren are safe. I remember how my mother and grandmother – even though they loved me – wouldn't listen when I tried to tell them that I didn't want to be left with my grandfather. Because of that I've always listened to what any child tells me. And I've acted on it.'

Both Beth and I lived with a secret that we kept to ourselves for many years. Throughout most of our adult life we carried on with our lives, trying not to remember the things from our childhood that haunted us. When I talk with Beth now, we often touch on the subject again. It's almost as if we have a small sister-hood going and can be free and easy with what we talk about. Beth asked me one day if I thought that time had healed me. I thought about it and said that I felt it had, but that my anger and hatred for my father still remained even though he was dead. Beth said she felt exactly the same.

'I'll never know why my grandfather did what he did, and I've accepted that I'll never know. But I'm still angry. And that's not a bad thing: my anger is what makes me determined to help change the world into a better place and help protect today's and tomorrow's children.'

I couldn't agree more.

4
Mike

I met Mike when I was seated next to him at a formal dinner that my husband and I had been invited to. It was a rather grand occasion and I was feeling a little uncomfortable – I'm much more at home in jeans than in sequins. So I was grateful to find that the man sitting next to me was friendly and easy to chat to. We swapped names, laughed about which knives and forks to use for what, and then got talking about our work and families.

Mike was in his late thirties, a good-looking, green-eyed, intelligent man, almost six feet tall, with wavy brown hair that curled over his collar. He was with his wife, Julia, a lovely-looking woman with a broad smile, and I introduced him to my husband Alan, who was on my other side. When Mike got up to have a word with the organisers during a break between courses, I noticed that he had a slight limp and wondered what had caused it.

Mike told me that he worked in insurance and Julia was in finance. They had a small daughter and lived on the outskirts of London. It was only towards the end of the meal that Mike told me he was a volunteer counsellor in his spare time for victims of domestic violence. I was intrigued and asked him whether that meant helping women whose partners had become violent. 'Yes,' he said, 'sometimes. But I counsel men too'. I asked whether he meant gay men whose partners had assaulted them. 'You're assuming that the perpetrators of domestic violence are always men.' He smiled. 'It's an easy mistake to make. But in fact there are plenty of women who are violent to their partners.'

I told him that I'd love to know more. 'I know women can be violent,' I said. 'But surely most men are stronger than their partners and can stop them if things get out of hand?'

'Not always,' Mike replied. 'And even when they are stronger, some men can't bring themselves to be violent or hit back. I know, because I was one of those men.'

I was curious, but there was no time to ask him about it: our conversation came to an end when the speeches were announced at the end of the dinner. Afterwards, as we were preparing to leave, Mike handed me his card and invited me to get in touch. I said I'd love to, and suggested that the four of us – Mike and Julia and me and Alan – should meet for dinner when Alan and I next came over to England.

Our chance came a few weeks later. I had liked Mike and was still curious about his story, so I called him and we arranged for the four of us to meet at a lovely pub beside the Thames just outside London, close to where Mike and Julia lived.

It was midsummer and we had a great evening, sitting outside as the light faded, eating our dinner, sharing a bottle of wine and watching ducklings on the water. It was almost dark when I plucked up the courage to ask Mike about his work in domestic violence and to tell me more of his own story.

'I see people one or two evenings a week,' he said. 'After what happened to me I know how isolated victims can be, and I wanted to do something to help. I don't mind telling you my story because I know now that the more we can talk about this kind of thing, the easier it is to prevent it. If men don't tell, then no one knows it's going on. I could have stopped what was happening to me much earlier than I did. But I was too ashamed to tell anyone – after all, most men, and probably a lot of women too, would laugh at the idea of a bloke being beaten up by his wife.'

I looked at Julia, but Mike laughed. 'No,' he said, 'it wasn't Julia. She's the one who's helped me to put my life back together again. It was my first wife, Sue, who was violent.'

Alan got another round in, as an almost full moon came out and Mike began to tell us his story.

Sue and I met when I had just left college and had got

my first job. I met her at a party and I was bowled over. She was very pretty and plenty of guys were after her, so I was flattered when she made a beeline for me.

We began dating and I was soon madly in love. Perhaps that's why I ignored some of Sue's less attractive qualities. Although she was lovely to look at and clever with it she was also petulant, spoilt and demanding. She had been very pampered by her well-off parents and she couldn't stand not getting what she wanted.

From the start she had the upper hand, while I ran in circles trying to please her. In those days I thought she was a fragile little thing. She was often ill and when she took to her bed I'd run out and get her flowers, perfume and cake, anything to cheer her up and make her smile again. My mum had been ill for a lot of my childhood and I learned to look after her. So I was used to being the 'fixer' trying to sort things out and make everything right and I just carried on with Sue like that.

When we got married I still thought I'd found my perfect woman. Her father made me promise to look after her and I swore that I would. We moved into a lovely little flat and at first life seemed good. But it didn't last long. Sue became more and more demanding, sulky and volatile. She had been used to being waited on day and night at home, and she had no intention of changing anything. Within a few months I was beginning to wonder what I'd let myself in for. Sue did almost nothing around the house when she got in from work – she had a job in public relations for a fashion house. She just lay on the sofa talking to her friends on the phone, waiting for me to do everything.

I was getting more and more fed-up and we began to have a lot of rows. I realised that I didn't want a fragile little princess, I wanted a real woman, a caring partner who'd meet me halfway and share the chores and the fun. But that wasn't Sue's style.

One day, after I refused to go to the shops and get her something she wanted, she threw a vase at me. It only just missed, smashing into the wall beside my head. I was really shocked: I had been brought up to believe that violence was wrong and to treat others – especially women – with politeness and respect. So flying vases were outside my experience.

I hoped it was a one-off, but it certainly wasn't. Sue began to be violent more and more often. She threw things, pushed and shoved me, hit me and threatened me. One time she grabbed a heavy frying pan and whacked me with it. She got me on the shoulder, and it came up in a huge black bruise.

When she saw what she'd done Sue was sorry, although she still managed to blame me, telling me that I'd provoked her. She promised not to do it again – but that promise only lasted two weeks.

Each attack grew more violent. Sue would totally lose it, shrieking and screaming at me, grabbing anything to hand and throwing it and damaging furniture and clothes.

I was much bigger than Sue, but I found her behaviour frightening and alarming. I just couldn't understand it. No one I knew had ever been violent – my family were all very quiet people – and I had no idea how to handle it.

As Sue got worse she began to injure me regularly. A couple of times I ended up in casualty but I always lied about how I'd got hurt because I was too embarrassed to admit that my wife had done it. Once my forehead was cut open when she threw a glass at me. I needed five stitches. Another time she hit me with a hockey stick – mine – and broke my finger.

I began to feel absolutely trapped, with no idea what to do. I never, ever, reacted violently to Sue's outbursts and tantrums – they just turned me right off. But my lack of reaction seemed to inflame her. I think she'd have been happier if I'd fought back or at least shouted at her. But I couldn't: the idea horrified me.

Strangely, the one thing that didn't occur to me was to leave her. I've asked myself why, and I think it was because of two things. First of all I was totally committed to the marriage. When I made my vows, I made them for life and I couldn't imagine going back on that. And secondly I really believed that if only I could find it there was a way to stop Sue and calm her down. And I thought that once I did everything would be fine.

I lied to myself in my effort to keep everything going. I told myself that Sue was temperamental and hot-headed, that she got a bit out of hand now and then.

But I never admitted to myself that actually she was uncontrollably violent, suffering bizarre mood swings and committing acts that would land most men in jail. I was guilty of total double standards: I made all kinds of allowances because she was a woman, a member of the 'gentler' sex, and persisted in the notion that it was supposed to be me looking after her, not her trying to bash my brains out.

The two of us led a miserable life. We had no mutual friends and didn't go out together. We just went to work, saw our separate friends – though I did so less and less – and then at home we either argued or avoided one another. Once in a while we managed to have a pleasant time together, like curling up on the sofa to watch TV, but that became increasingly rare.

I realised that Sue despised me: she would shout at me that I wasn't a proper man and all kinds of other insults. I guess she thought a 'proper' man would throw her over his shoulder or pin her down – I don't really know what she wanted. But whatever it was, I didn't fit the bill and, believe me, I didn't feel like much of a man when I had to spend a couple of hours two or three times a week ducking and diving to avoid her missiles or her fists.

One of the things that kept me with her was that Sue apologised after each incident. She would say that she didn't know what came over her, that she hadn't meant to hurt me, that she just wanted us to start afresh and so on. I'd listen and, for a long time, I believed her. But it wore thin in the end.

I asked her to go for help many times. I thought that a doctor or a counsellor or even a friend might help her. I wondered if she had a hormonal imbalance, or whether an anger-management course would help. But Sue rejected the idea of telling anyone at all. I think that was because she wasn't willing to take responsibility for what she was doing. She blamed me, or the day she'd had at work, or her boss, or the weather – anything but herself.

Things came to a head when Sue pushed me down the stairs one day. I can't even remember what she was shouting about at the time, but whatever it was she was furious and as I went to go downstairs to get away from her she shoved me so hard that I fell the whole way down. Our stairs had no carpet – they were wooden and very hard. I landed awkwardly and I knew that my leg was badly hurt. I asked Sue to get an ambulance, and when she saw what she'd done she was frightened and called for help. She tried to get into the ambulance with me, playing the anxious wife, but I told them I didn't want her there and they asked her to follow by car. X-rays showed that my leg was badly broken in two places and my hip was fractured too. I had two operations and spent a month in hospital. While I was there I had a lot of time to think. I knew I didn't want to stay with Sue: I was suicidal at the thought of going home and carrying on in the same way. And I was pretty sure that if I didn't kill myself, she'd end up killing me.

One day, in the hospital common room, I saw a leaflet about domestic violence. I picked it up, read it – and did a double take when it said that women could be violent and men could be victims too. At that moment I realised that Sue wasn't just troubled, or hot-headed: she was violent, dangerous and abusive.

Sue was visiting me regularly, being honey-sweet and telling me that she was going to look after me. One of the nurses even said to me 'Isn't your wife lovely?' I thought, 'If only you knew.'

The next time Sue came I told her that I wasn't coming home. At first she didn't believe me. Then, when she saw that I meant it, she looked at me as though she could kill me. She reached under the bed-clothes and pinched me, as hard as she could. Then she got up and marched out.

The next day I got a call from her father, saying that Sue was very upset. He had a real go at me, claiming that I had let him down and asking how could I think of leaving her. He demanded to know whether I was seeing someone else. I realised Sue had told him a pack of lies. I kept my cool and said there was no one else, but that I wouldn't tolerate Sue's behaviour any more. I didn't go into details, just left it at that.

Two days later I left hospital and went to stay with an old friend. He knew nothing about my troubles with Sue – I just told him that the marriage was breaking down and he offered me a sofa to sleep on for as long as I needed it. The next day, while he was at work, I called the domestic-violence hotline. The woman on the other end was really sympathetic and invited me to come in and see someone. I did, and I was given a lot of good advice. But I was disappointed that there wasn't a man I could talk to: all the staff at the centre were women. Still, they were lovely. They didn't make any judgements, just offered me counselling and practical support.

I saw the counsellor and it was a relief to be able to admit at last that I'd been battered by my wife for over two years. I'm not ashamed to admit that I cried a lot. I was so sad that my marriage had failed and I felt so hurt by Sue's behaviour.

It took me a few months to get my life back together. My leg healed slowly, but I was left with a limp as a permanent reminder not just of Sue's behaviour but of how willing I had been to put up with it. I went back to work, found a flat to rent and made sure that Sue didn't have the address or my phone number. Her only contact for me was my mobile and I kept our conversations brief. I told her I wanted a divorce and that she needed help. Perhaps I got through, because she told me that she was going for counselling. But then again, that could have been just one of Sue's lines. We got divorced quickly – no kids, so it was simple, thank goodness. I let her have most of what we'd shared; I didn't care, as long as I was free.

My counsellor told me that I'd be surprised by how

many men get battered by their female partners, and it made me think. While I had been a victim I had never thought that it could be happening to someone else as well. I felt so alone. Yet there were other men out there, just like me, probably all of them feeling just as alone as I was. And men, even more than women, find it hard to open up and talk about what they feel or the painful things that are going on in their lives. We're brought up to keep it all inside and put on a brave front, but that's not always helpful.

I decided to train part-time as a counsellor and work with abused men. And I set up a group for male victims of domestic violence. I encourage them to get help, and to see that they needn't feel shame. Just because you're a man it doesn't mean that you can't be a victim.

It's seven years since Sue and I divorced, and five years ago I met Julia. She's everything I could hope for in a partner. We talk, we share and we treat one another with kindness. Of course we row, but neither of us is ever violent or aggressive and we sort things out by talking. We've got our gorgeous daughter Lydia and I couldn't be happier.

When I was married to Sue I couldn't imagine a time ever coming when I would be happy again. I dreaded each day, and had to drag myself through it. Living with almost daily violence saps your energy, your courage and your self-belief. But what I learned is that by doing something about it and saying 'enough' you can win all those things back.

*   *   *

I thanked Mike for telling us his story. I learned a lot from listening to him. I had been guilty of thinking that only women were real victims of violence, and that men could always look after themselves. Yet hearing this honest man's story made me understand that there *are* men in this world who would never lift a finger in anger or violence towards a woman, even when she is attacking them.

Mike was a gentle man, a peaceful man and a kind man. And in my book that didn't make him a wimp. It made him a hero.

5
Abbi

Abbi was a fellow mum at my daughter Martine's school. We got to know each other in passing and in time became good friends, dropping into one another's homes for coffee or getting together with our girls for tea after school. I wanted to include Abbi's story because it highlights a loophole in the law and the terrible injustice that some victims of assault can suffer. What happened to Abbi was appalling yet her attacker was given a minimal sentence, which was all that the law allowed. Abbi was badly let down by the system and on top of the physical injury, mental anguish and disastrous consequences of what had happened to her she was left to live with the awful injustice and the knowledge that her attacker was soon at large again.

As we chatted at the school gates Abbi and I soon discovered that we were both single parents. Abbi's daughter Poppy was six, the same age as Martine, and Abbi herself was about my age.

Abbi was a very proud mum, I could see that the minute I walked into her modest but very clean flat. There were pictures of her daughter everywhere. It was a common bond between us, for I had pictures of Martine everywhere too. We chatted a lot about our lives with our daughters and our hopes and ambitions for them. I told Abbi about Martine's father, who would come and go, always causing trouble when he was around. She was very supportive, offering help if I needed it and a place to go if I ever felt threatened.

Abbi was not a stunning beauty, but she was attractive and had a lovely way about her. Curiosity got the better of me one day and I asked her why she had no one special in her life. Abbi looked at me and the colour faded from her cheeks as she nervously tucked a lock of her brown hair behind her ears.

'Oh, you know, Jen, since Poppy's dad, I felt I couldn't trust anyone again. And besides, I'm so busy with Poppy that I don't get the chance to get out and about and meet anyone.'

I suggested a girls' night out with some of my other friends, but Abbi seemed adamant that it wasn't for her. I decided not to press her any further and once I dropped the subject Abbi seemed to relax.

Things continued pretty much the same for the next few weeks. Whenever we could, Abbi and I would meet up for morning coffee and a chat and I enjoyed our time together and looked forward to seeing her. Life wasn't easy as a single parent twenty-five years ago and for both of us things were tough. There was very little money about – I worked as a barmaid in the evenings and Abbi had a part-time job in a shop, and we both struggled to get by. But there was always laughter and the help and support of good friends.

One day, another friend of mine asked me to help out at the local café, washing up. I was only too glad and for the next two weeks I had a bit of extra money coming in, which was great. While I was working there I had to miss my coffee mornings with Abbi and didn't get the chance to see her. After my stint at the café finished I looked for Abbi at school, hoping to catch her for a coffee.

Suddenly, another friend scurried round the corner with Poppy and her own two children in tow. As she dropped the children at the gate and watched them go in I asked her where Abbi was. She told me that Abbi had been unwell and depressed for a week, so I headed straight off to her flat. When Abbi opened the door, I was taken aback by her ashen face. I asked her what on earth was wrong. She said nothing, but stood to one side to let me in. I could see that she was in a bad way, so I took my coat off and then put the kettle on. Abbi just stood and watched me. She had always been an introvert, appearing timid and shy, especially to those who didn't know her well, but now she seemed almost to have disappeared inside herself.

I made the tea and we both sat down at the kitchen table. I told her that I was concerned about her but that she didn't have to tell me anything if she didn't want to. But to my surprise Abbi looked straight at me and said, 'I'm desperate to say something, I feel I can't go on carrying this on my own. You see, Jen, he's out and free and I'm terrified. If anyone can understand, it's you.'

I had no idea what she was talking about. I looked at her pale face, and asked her, 'Who's out and who's free?'

'I suppose I knew it would happen one day. But five years is a long time and, well, I put off thinking about it for so long that now it's all come as a bit of a shock.'

I still couldn't make sense of what Abbi was saying, so I prompted her again.

'Five years ago, something awful happened that changed my life for ever. He was sent to prison and now he's out and I'm scared, Jen.'

'Is it Poppy's dad?' I asked.

'No, Poppy's dad left after what happened, because I couldn't let him come near me any more. This is another man. He was just someone I knew to say hello to whenever I passed him. But in fifteen minutes one sunny afternoon, he changed my life for ever.'

I told Abbi that if she wanted to tell me the whole story I would be happy to listen. She held her cup with both hands and started to sip her tea. Then she placed the cup on the kitchen table and stood up. She went to the kitchen window and gazed out, seemingly lost in thought, and began to talk.

Before that man changed everything, I had a good life. I had known Steve since I was sixteen – he was my only boyfriend. We got married when I was nineteen and nine months later Poppy was born. We couldn't have been happier: we both loved kids and wanted a big family.

Life was really good for us. We'd moved into our own flat, Steve had lots of work, and we were blissful and happy – until that day just over six years ago.

Proud as Punch of my new baby and with the sun shining, I decided to take her for a walk in the park. She was just about four months old and already smiling and I loved it when people stopped to admire her. There were quite a few people around that day. Mothers and their toddlers feeding the ducks, people jogging and even a few fishermen trying their luck in the lake. There was a lovely breeze and all the flowers were blooming – the air smelled wonderful.

I had a skip in my step as I wheeled Poppy along in her smart new pram. I decided to have a proper walk and take the long way round, past the lake and the bandstand. Halfway along I sat down on a bench to have a cigarette, and was just watching the world go by when he came and sat next to me. He was vaguely familiar, and I realised that I knew him from the darts team at our local pub. He asked after Steve and looked at Poppy in her pram. It was all so normal, until suddenly he took the handle of the pram and said, 'If you know what's good for you, you'll get up without a fuss and go over to the bushes.'

I panicked and asked him what on earth he was talking about. 'Just do as I say,' he said in a low, menacing voice. 'She's not a bad-looking kid and you don't want anything to happen to her, now, do you?' I looked around and realised that there was no one in view. I was on the other side of the park from all the other mums and children and I couldn't even hear anyone. I asked him if he wanted money and started to search in my bag, but he got agitated and raised his voice as he ordered me over to a small area that was thick with bushes.

The pram, with Poppy in it, was left by the bench as he grabbed my arm and led me away. By this time I was terrified and praying that nothing would happen to my baby. The man threw me to the ground and began ripping at my clothes and telling me to take my shorts and knickers off. I begged him to let me go, but he just laughed, and kept pointing to the pram that was still in view.

He suddenly put his arm around my neck and forced me to the ground. 'Let's see what you have to offer,' he said as he forced my legs apart and pushed his fingers inside me.

Everything seemed unreal. I tried to turn my head away to avoid seeing his ugly face. I could see movement on the other side of the bushes and I could hear muffled voices. It was a bus stop and people were standing there, waiting for the bus. 'Help me,' I pleaded, but as the words left my mouth I felt the most agonising pain rip through my body, as though I had been torn apart, and I blacked out.

When I recovered consciousness and realised that he had gone my immediate thoughts were for Poppy. I looked towards the pram, which mercifully was still there, and I could make out two women looking into it and talking to my baby. I tried to move but the pain was too much, and as I looked down at the lower half of my body all I could see was blood.

With all my strength, I called out, 'Help me, please. For God's sake, help me.' The two women came hurrying over. I heard a gasp, and one of them said, 'Run for help – get an ambulance.' There were footsteps, running, and then more voices – she must have gone to the people at the bus stop. The first woman was kneeling beside me, trying to reassure me. I could hear her saying, 'It's OK, sweetheart, help is on the way, your baby is safe and well.' I looked at her and saw tears in her eyes as she said, 'My God, who would do such a thing?'

The next few hours were a blur. I remember the ambulance arriving and I remember the terrible pain I felt as they lifted me onto the stretcher. I must have passed out for some time because the next thing I was aware of was Steve touching my arm to wake me gently.

Apparently I had been in the operating room for three hours. Do you know what that bastard did to me, Jen? He hadn't raped me – that would have been too simple. He'd inserted his whole arm into my vagina and ripped me apart from front to back.

How could anyone do something so terrible? He must have really hated women to want to hurt one so badly.

The doctors told me that I would need several more operations – reconstructive surgery. They also told me that I wouldn't be able to have any more children – I was just too damaged.

That was a terrible blow, for me and for Steve. We just sobbed together. I couldn't take it in that in such a short time I had been injured so badly. I was in hospital for weeks and when I came home everything had changed. Despite all the terrible injuries he had caused me, they are nothing compared to what I lost after the attack. For months I was barely able to function, I was in constant pain and because of my injuries I was unable to have sex or even to pee properly. I felt I was no longer a woman and it ruined my marriage.

I knew Steve loved me and would stay with me no matter what the situation was. But I loved him so much that I couldn't allow him to stay, knowing that I couldn't make love to him or have any more children. I was afraid that if he stayed it would be out of pity. I felt he was too young to throw his future away on me. In the end I made it impossible for him to stay. I told him I didn't love or want him any more, which wasn't true. It broke my heart to let him go, but I wanted him to have the life we had once planned together.

Steve agreed not to see Poppy as we both felt it was all too painful. It probably wasn't fair to her, but I knew that I wouldn't be able to bear to see him, knowing I still loved him.

Steve left a year after the attack and after that I just got quietly on with life as best I could. I had several more operations – my mum took Poppy each time – and I'm better than I was, but I'm still a mess down there. I haven't even let myself think about another relationship – who'd want me in this state? That's why I always turn down the opportunities to go out with the girls. I think to myself, what's the point?

The attacker was arrested and was charged very quickly. I was relieved, thinking he'd go away for a long time. But because he didn't *technically* rape me – he didn't insert his penis into me – it was classed as assault, which is a more minor offence, even though the injury was far worse than an actual rape would have caused. He got the maximum sentence, but that was only five years.

Now he's out again, and it feels like only yesterday that he was sent down. Knowing he's out there is bringing it all back.

I moved away after the split with Steve. The attacker doesn't know where I live now, or that Steve and I are not together, but the thought that he is back out and walking around, a free man, makes my blood run cold. The police called me and they have assured me that he is miles away from where I live. That's true, but he's gone back to the area where I – and he – used to live and my mum still lives there. She phoned to say that she had seen him, and that he'd had the cheek to smile at her. My mum was outraged and as she talked about it all those terrible memories just came back. I feel scared and threatened, and fearful for Poppy.

Some people have accused me of being overprotective of Poppy, but she really is all I have now and I still feel so very alone. Now he's out I feel that I daren't leave the house.

Abbi smiled at me, and reached for a tissue to blow her nose.

'I don't intend to give up, Jen. I know I have to make the right choices and the right decisions for Poppy. Did I ever tell you that I have family up in Scotland? My mum's sister lives there with her family, and I've been thinking of moving up there. They own a guest house and need help and I thought it would be a great place for Poppy to grow up. My aunt has grandchildren around the same age as her and it will give me something to do, instead of hiding away. I've even thought about of doing a course in hotel management.'

I told Abbi that I thought her plans sounded wonderful, but that I would really miss her. I knew it would be pointless trying to persuade her to stay – why should she when the monster who attacked her was walking around not far away?

I was shocked that Abbi had been given so little

help: she hadn't been offered counselling or any other type of support and had simply been left to recover from her physical and mental traumas alone.

Moving away is not always the answer, but in some cases I think it's necessary. In a matter of weeks Abbi had made up her mind and packed up, ready to go to Scotland. When I saw her she was pleased and excited about her new start. For the first time in five years she could see a light and some hope. Saying goodbye was emotional. We had become close friends and so had our girls, but Abbi invited us to stay with them in Scotland and I promised to take her up on it.

In the weeks that followed I missed Abbi a great deal and thought of her often. So I was delighted when a letter arrived from Scotland. Abbi spoke of her new life and said she was really enjoying herself. She had gone ahead and enrolled in night school to study hotel management and she said she was loving every minute. Poppy had settled in at the little primary school and had lots of friends. In the last line of her warm and hopeful letter, Abbi wrote:

'I needed to change and I have. I don't have to look over my shoulder any more, and I'm looking forward to the future.'

I did visit Abbi in Scotland and found her more peaceful and happy than I had ever seen her in London. And twenty-five years on we are still in touch. Poppy is happily married to a farmer and has three wonderful children and Abbi is happy as a senior manager of a large hotel. She has her own lovely home and is surrounded by her grandchildren. The struggle with her physical problems continue, and she recently had to undergo further surgery to her bladder. But she takes it all in her stride with incredible resilience and strength.

As for the man who attacked her, Abbi heard a few years back that he had died in a car crash. Rough justice, but for Abbi a kind of justice nonetheless. As she said to me at the time, 'I try not to wish anyone ill, Jen. It was only after I heard that he'd died that I felt a kind of relief and realised that after all this time I was still angry. I can't help feeling that the world is better off without him.'

I can only agree.

I'm glad to say that the law is more flexible now and a serious assault such as the attack on Abbi carries a potentially higher sentence. It is also much more likely now that Abbi would be referred to victim support and offered counselling and practical help.

As it is, Abbi managed her recovery alone, and every time I see her I am reminded that, quiet and shy as she is, she has a remarkable and humbling degree of inner strength.

6
Rani

I like to think that I am quite an astute person and can pick up on another person's distress or discomfort. But with Rani I hadn't a clue. Maybe because my own family were scattered and not very close I was blind to the misery of a young woman who had lost all that was dear to her. I had long since let go of any notion of my own family being united and was only too happy to escape from my parents. But Rani was brought up to believe that family was everything and that the honour of and respect for her family must come before any personal wishes or dreams.

Yet when the demands of her family came into conflict with her longing to make her own choices and be her own person, Rani was torn. Should she do as she was ordered and lose all joy in life, or should she follow her heart and be free? She knew that her decision would dictate the course of the rest of her life.

Rani's story is about a different kind of abuse: the cruelty of parents who wish to force a child to bend to their will, with no regard for who she is or what might be right for her as an individual in her own right. Rani's parents brought her up within their own culture while living in Britain, where she was surrounded by the influences of a very different lifestyle. All around her Rani saw girls who were free to choose their own direction in life: who they married, whether they married at all and how they lived. And of course she wanted the freedom that they had, not only to marry the man of her choice but to use her brain and live the way she wished.

I first met Rani some years ago when I went to work for my local authority. I was employed as a cashier, taking council tax payments soon after they were introduced. Rani was employed behind the scenes, but as she spoke a number of Indian dialects she often came out to assist us and our customers when we needed an interpreter.

Rani was a very beautiful girl. Her long black hair was usually pinned back to reveal a beautiful face with large almond-shaped eyes and a lovely smile. Although she was Indian, Rani's dress and attitudes were very Western and she appeared to be a girl who had effortlessly transcended the barrier between two cultures.

We often bumped into each other at lunchtime and would sometimes sit together in the cafeteria of the Co-Op store near work, having a cup of coffee. We usually chatted about work and rarely spoke of our personal lives until one day I mentioned something that had happened to me in the past. I didn't tell Rani about my childhood but I did mention how dictatorial my father had been.

I could see that Rani was lost in thought, but when I asked her if she was daydreaming she replied, 'No, more like a day nightmare.' I asked her if she was OK and if she needed to talk. Her hands trembling, she lit up her third cigarette in ten minutes. I assured her that she didn't have to say anything to me if she didn't want to, but she said, 'No, actually Jenny, I'd like to.

'I wasn't born in this area, I was born in Bradford. There's a very strong Indian community there, you know, and I was raised in a large terraced house with my two sisters and three brothers. The family was very close and, as is usual with Indian families, we had lots of aunties, uncles and cousins living nearby.

'My father was very strict and insisted that we all should have a good education. My elder sister Mina was doing incredibly well and was hoping to go to medical school and become a doctor. Then one day after we got home from school Dad put paid to her dreams by announcing that a suitable husband had been found for her and that she was to leave for India in the following month.

'We were all speechless. Despite our lives in the UK and our hopes and ambitions, my father still wanted us to stick to the old traditions and have arranged marriages. My mother quietly nodded in agreement with my father and within a month Mina was packed off to India. I haven't seen her since. I believe she has two children now, but since I left Bradford we have been unable to stay in touch.'

I asked why she was not in touch with her sister.

'I can't speak with any of my family, except my brother, not now, not ever,' Rani said. 'You see, I gave everything up to be myself. I couldn't stay, knowing that my fate would be the same as Mina's. I was the second-eldest daughter, and I knew that my parents were planning the same thing for me and that I would be sent to India to marry a stranger, become part of his family and spend the rest of my life doing the bidding of my in-laws.'

She took a deep breath. 'The truth is, Rani is not even my real name. I changed it, as I changed everything about myself, to make sure that I couldn't be found. I brought shame on my family and if they found me I would be punished, possibly by death.'

I thought of the stories that I had read about Indian girls being killed by their fathers, brothers and male cousins after they refused to enter arranged marriages. It was hard to believe that anyone could feel so strongly about a principle that they would be willing to murder their own child, but I knew it happened. Had Rani really been at such risk?

'Yes,' she replied. 'For weeks after Mina had gone, I struggled to come to terms with losing her. We had been so close, I missed her terribly and I couldn't forget her grief and tears in the weeks before she was sent to India. And once she'd gone it was as if she'd been banished from her family and everything she had known.

'I knew that I could never go through that. Mina had submitted to our parents' will, like a good daughter, but it wasn't for me. So I started to plan my escape. Can you begin to imagine how this was for me? I was only sixteen. Each day I would go to school and not eat lunch in order to save what little money I could. Every evening, I would sit and eat dinner with my family, knowing that I was deceiving them and that the time would soon come when I would never see them again. I felt such misery and guilt. But I could see no other way.' So began Rani's story of abuse and heartbreak.

I respected the beliefs handed down by many generations in the culture of my birth. But I didn't feel like an Indian girl – at least, not fully. I was living in Britain, going to a comprehensive school and most of my friends were from a Western culture. I liked pop music, pretty dresses, good books. I was clever, like Mina, I'd passed my GCSEs with good grades and knew that I wanted to work. How could I give it all up for a life of obedience to a culture I no longer felt part of?

Sadly, I couldn't talk of any of this with my family. My parents would have been shocked and outraged and would probably have put me on a plane to India the next day.

Thankfully I had Sarah, my best friend, and together we began to hatch my escape plan. Sarah knew a few people down in the south of England, so I decided to go there.

As I saved and planned and prepared, it was agony deceiving my family and knowing that I would never have their love and support. I used to look at my little sister and my brothers and try not to cry, thinking about how badly I'd miss them.

One day my younger brother, Chandresh, noticed my stricken face and asked me what was wrong. I started to cry and told him that I could not face my future the way our parents wanted it to be. I was very close to Chandresh and he seemed to understand and even offered to help me. So I decided to confide in him about my plan to escape. He understood and promised to keep it secret. I felt happier, knowing that at least one family member would not abandon me.

I knew that education would help me to get a good job. My A levels were looming and I engrossed myself in my books, determined to do well. I had always been good at figures and dreamed of going to university, but first I had to get good enough grades. Each evening I would pore over my books and when I needed to dream a little I would envisage my life as a well-educated woman, living my dream in London.

Time passed quickly, although sometimes, knowing what lay ahead, I wished it would stand still so that I could stay with my family. I passed my exams with top grades and the family were elated that I had done so well. I couldn't help wondering why my parents cared, since they weren't expecting me to go to university or even to work. I think that in their eyes it simply made me more attractive as a prospective wife.

I had been grateful that they'd let me take the exams at all, since Mina had been shipped off before her A levels. I knew the day must be coming when my turn would come, and sure enough, a couple of weeks after my results came through my father sat me down to tell me that now was the time for us all to think about a suitable marriage for me.

My protests went unheard, as I had known they would. I looked at my mother, hoping that she might be on my side, but she stood behind my father, nodding her acceptance as he spoke. Chandresh, sitting nearby, caught my eye and gave me a reassuring smile.

My father was saying that he had two possible suitors in mind and wanted me to see their photographs. I decided that, since I would never change his mind, I had better play along and I agreed to look at them. The photos of two strange men, both of them far older than me and unattractive, convinced me that I had to go ahead with my plan.

Sarah had been wonderful and a true friend and with her help I was able to arrange a place to stay in Watford, just north of London, and obtain an interview for a job as a trainee accountant with a local firm. For some time, before my exams, I had been taking one item of clothing at a time to school in my book bag and Sarah had been packing them away for me in a suitcase which she kept ready at her house.

In early October my father announced that he had chosen a husband for me and had arranged for me to go to India in a month's time, so I had no time to waste. The night before I left I sat at dinner with my family for the last time. I found it almost impossible to eat. My mind was racing – I felt despair and excitement at the same time. I couldn't quite believe that I wouldn't see them again. My mother asked me if I was all right and, afraid that I would break down, I had to leave the table, pretending I had a headache, and go to bed. As I left the table, my mother stood up and came and put her arms around me I felt a terrible pain in my heart. I loved her so, and as she hugged me I hugged her back, tighter and longer than necessary.

I spent the whole night sobbing into my pillow. As the sun rose, I pulled myself together, splashed cold water on my face and got dressed. This was really it. I looked around the room I had shared with my sister Mina and thought of our happy times together.

I thought of my parents who I knew loved me, despite their plans for me, and I thought of my sister and my brothers, especially Chandresh, whom I would miss so much. Did I really know what I was doing, going into the world alone at just eighteen and beginning a totally new life? I knew I had to try.

I told my parents that I had arranged to go round to Sarah's to give her back some books I had borrowed. They agreed and I left the house, taking only my handbag and coat. When I reached Sarah's home she was waiting for me. We went up to her bedroom and went through the next stages of my escape. The train left at 1.25 p.m. and Sarah's friends had agreed to pick me up when I arrived in Watford.

Sarah handed me my suitcase. I had managed to put into it some clothes, along with a few small mementoes and photos of my family. From now on that small case and its contents would be all that I owned in the world. In my bag I had a train ticket and a little money which I hoped would be enough to keep me going until I got a job.

Sarah reassured me that the family I was going to would look after me and that all would be well. It was almost time to leave and as we looked at each other we both began to cry. We hugged and I wondered when I would see my friend again. We had agreed that she wouldn't contact me for a while in case my family – or hers – found out. We hadn't told Sarah's parents of our plan in case they felt they had to tell my parents the truth. As I left Sarah's house and made my way to the bus stop I felt uneasy. I had the feeling that I was being watched and I glanced over my shoulder several times. But there was no one there and eventually I told myself that I was just being stupid.

As I sat on the bus my heart was thumping so hard that I thought it would burst through my blouse. I gripped the little bag that held all my worldly goods and gazed at the faces of the other passengers, wondering what they would think if they knew what I was doing.

The station was teeming with people checking time-tables and buying tickets. I looked at people kissing loved ones and felt a lump in my throat. Almost sick with nerves, I made my way to the platform and sat on a bench, waiting. There were only five minutes to go until I stepped on the train and into my new life. An argument at the ticket gate became quite heated as voices were raised. I looked up.

To my horror I saw my father, shouting and arguing with the ticket inspector. A moment later he pushed his way through the gate and onto the platform and began looking around.

Panic set in. My mind was racing but I felt glued to my seat. What happened next is all a bit of a blur in my memory. I remember being dragged up from my seat and pulled along the platform. I was shouting for someone to help me but no one did. In fact, some seemed to find the whole thing amusing.

My father's face was enraged as he frogmarched me to the car and shoved me into the back. As I sat, flanked by my aunt on one side and my uncle on the other, I could see my mother's reflection in the mirror. My aunt was talking non-stop, but my mother sat silent, her face grim. I felt trapped, helpless and very frightened. What were they going to do to me?

When we reached home, it seemed that all our relatives were there. The house was full and as I was led in everyone began shouting at me, telling me what an ungrateful and disloyal daughter I was.

There was a sea of angry faces and a barrage of angry words.

I felt as though my head was about to explode. My arms were being held as if I was going to bolt if they let go and the shouting voices felt as though they were banging on my temples. All I could think was, how had they known? Who had betrayed me? And what was going to happen to me now?

As I looked around the room I saw Chandresh, his head bowed and his eyes lowered. He raised his face and looked at me, his expression one of despair and anguish, and suddenly I knew who had betrayed me. Then I felt my legs give way and I must have fainted.

When I awoke, after my faint, I was in my room. It was very dark, the curtains were drawn and I could hardly see a thing. I had no idea what time it was or whether it was dark or light outside. Puzzled, I got up and went to open the curtains. As I did, I gasped. Behind them, across the window frame, planks of wood had been nailed so that there was barely any space for natural light to come in. I could see that it was dark outside so I went over to the door to find the light switch.

The bright overhead light and its shade had been replaced with a gloomy bulb which gave very little light. Looking around, I realised that my room had been completely transformed. Gone were my posters, books, clothing and other possessions. In fact, there was nothing in it apart from the bed.

Slowly it dawned on me that my room had been turned into a cell. I tried the door, but even before I turned the handle I knew that it wouldn't open. I felt total panic. I screamed until I was hoarse for someone to let me out and banged on the door as hard as I could, but no one came. Eventually I slumped back on the bed, too weary and drained even to cry. This was to be my punishment, then, for disobedience. I wondered how long I would have to stay locked away.

I am not even sure how long I was forced to live like that. For the next few weeks I stayed in that room twenty-four hours a day. My toilet was a bucket and I was passed food and drink through the door by a relative. I didn't see my mother, father, sister or any of my brothers. Twice a day I was given a bowl of water and some soap, so that I could wash, and my toilet bucket was emptied. No one spoke to me, despite my pleas, and for the rest of the time I was left alone. I barely even knew whether it was day or night and I lost track of the days that passed.

I can't remember how often I cried and wished to die – it was many, many times. A lot of the time I just lay and stared at the ceiling. I had absolutely nothing to do, no book to read, no paper to write on. I knew that I had been left to think about my sins and pray for forgiveness. I did pray, but for release, although I had very little hope. I believed I would be killed or, if I was lucky, taken straight to the airport and put on a plane to India and a forced marriage.

Often I wondered whether I would go mad, locked up like that, in silence and with nothing to occupy my mind. It was literally torture. I tried to make up little games or rhymes to keep myself sane, but as time went by I became more and more depressed and despairing.

Then one day I heard the key turn in the lock and Chandresh put his head around the door. He came in and sat on the edge of the bed. Then he began to cry and asked me for forgiveness.

He explained that my parents had become suspicious, asking him over and over again if he knew anything about what I was up to. They had noticed how nervous and edgy I was and had guessed that something was going on. Chandresh had been put under enormous pressure: he had finally broken down on the morning of my escape and told them that I was running away.

The whole family had been called together to support my parents in stopping me from shaming the family. Relatives had gone to anywhere I might be, including Sarah's house, and I had been followed from there to the station. From there they had called my father, who had come to get me.

My relatives had been devastated that I had defied them and gone against their wishes. Chandresh told me that their plan was to force me into submission by keeping me prisoner until they could arrange for me to be sent to India and married into a suitable family. He hugged me and told me that he would help me. The family had all gone to a celebration and he had told them he felt unwell and had been left behind and given strict instructions not to come near me. I was surprised that they trusted him, but he told me that he had been punished last time for not telling them sooner about my plan to run away, and since then he had convinced them that he was sorry and was on their side.

I was touched that Chandresh was willing to aid me. Goodness knows what they might do to him for helping me to escape. But he was willing to face the consequences and I had to go. If I didn't take this chance there might never be another; I would be taken from my prison straight to the plane and that would be that.

Chandresh urged me to hurry. He gave me some of his clothes and as I dressed he told me that he had some money for me. I scraped my hair back and put on a baseball cap. In my brother's clothes I hoped I could pass for a boy if anyone saw me leave the house. Then he hurried me out of the back door and we ran all the way to the bus station. He left me there, with a hasty hug and a promise to stay in touch, and I boarded the next coach to London.

Sitting by the window as we sped down the motorway, I stared into the night at the lights of the oncoming traffic. I wondered what on earth would happen to me. I still felt dazed from being locked up for so long, and I had nothing but the clothes I was wearing and the few pounds that Chandresh had given me.

He had talked to Sarah, who had been devastated when she'd learned what had happened. She had sent me her love, and a message to say that I could still go to her friends in Watford. Chandresh had given me a piece of paper with their address on it, which was in my pocket. So I had somewhere to start.

I arrived in Watford, exhausted and still in shock, early the next morning. I was scared when I knocked on the door of Sarah's friends' house. What if they didn't want me around, especially once they saw how odd I looked and realised that I had nothing? But in fact they were kind, lovely people who took me in and gave me a home for the next few weeks, while I began my new life.

That was seven years ago and things have gone well for me since. I got a job and then a university place and got my degree. I made new friends, and after university I found a good job and a flat to share.

I've travelled to places I had only previously dreamed of and I even backpacked to India where, in a funny sort of way, I understood what my parents wanted for me, though I knew it would never be for me. Two years ago I went skiing and met Kevin and we're planning to marry next year. So I've been blessed.

My only sadness is that I no longer have my family. Although I felt very angry about what my parents put me through when they imprisoned me I still miss them all so much and would love to get in touch. I'd love to know what my little sister and brothers are doing and whether they are happy, but I know that isn't possible. Chandresh and Sarah stay in touch and they've told me that my parents consider me dead and so do my sister and brothers.

It wasn't just me they cut off. When they found out what Chandresh had done they threw him out and they haven't spoken to him since. He passes them in the street sometimes, but they walk past without even acknowledging him. He is sad about it too. But he has found happiness – with Sarah. They got together after I left and have been a couple ever since, and that makes me very happy. They come to visit me in London and it's always wonderful to see them.

Rani smiled. 'I could never have imagined my brother and my friend getting together at the time. But then, how many things ever do turn out the way we think?'

'Not many,' I agreed. I wondered whether Rani thought her parents would ever soften, with time.

'No.' She shook her head. 'I don't believe they will. Once they decide someone is effectively dead, they stick to it. I wonder sometimes if my mother misses me and Chandresh. It's not easy to lose two of your children. But she will be loyal to my father no matter what, and he will not bend. I have lost them.'

Had she ever regretted choosing to become a Western woman, I wondered?

'No.' Rani smiled. 'I don't regret it. I love my life and

the freedom I have. And I'm not completely Western: I still respect my roots and some of our traditions. I remember my mother's Indian recipes and often make them – they are something I can pass on to my own children.

'I will never forget my home or my family – there will always be sadness for me when I think of them. I wish I hadn't had to choose between them and a future. I try to understand my parents, but I will never be able to completely forgive them for what they put me through. I don't want to remember how long I was locked away in that room with nothing and treated like an animal because I was born a girl. I still can't stomach sex discrimination and the way women are sometimes made to feel, just because we're female.'

As Rani and I walked back to the office I thought about her story. She suffered so much fear, loss, grief and shame, not to mention the dreadful time she spent imprisoned in her own room, all because her parents were so rigid and stubborn in their beliefs that they would rather lose her than respect her free will. Their cruelty towards her – and it *was* cruelty, even though it was inflicted in the name of tradition – was unforgivable.

Rani and I became good friends. She invited me over to try some of her mother's recipes and they were delicious. The following year I went to her wedding – a wonderful mix of East and West. Rani deserved peace and happiness and she found it with Kevin: she was a truly happy bride. Chandresh and Sarah were there and they too seemed really happy. For Rani and her brother, good came out of suffering: I was so glad for them.

Rani and I have stayed friends – she recently helped me celebrate my fiftieth birthday. She is as beautiful as ever and still happily married to Kevin. They have three lovely children, two of them girls who, Rani told me proudly, are at college and living their lives to the full.

7
Elsie

Elsie's story goes back to the days when I was very young. She was a neighbour of my beloved Auntie and a lovely, kind woman whom I'd known for years and who suddenly confided in me one day when I was in my teens. It was a one-off moment that stayed with me until I met her again, years later, and heard the end of the story.

Elsie was old school, an old-fashioned woman who believed that marriage was for ever, no matter what, and that she must endure whatever her husband did to her. I wanted to tell her story because in many ways I think Elsie is typical of those women through the ages who, because of society's traditions, have suffered in silence. When such women do find the courage to speak out things begin to change for the better. I hope that today no woman feels she has to suffer as Elsie did and that women who are being abused in a marriage know there is always someone to listen and offer support, and there is always a way out.

In the days when I first met Elsie, when I was a small girl, my home was a frightening and ugly place to be.

We lived in a flat that was so dirty it was vermin-infested and stinking.

Suffice it to say that our parents were completely incapable of cleaning or running a home. There was seldom any food in the larder and we often went hungry. If we were lucky we'd get jam sandwiches or some chips for tea and we usually went to school with no breakfast. There was never any money for coal in those pre-central heating days – so we froze in winter. We'd hear the coalman delivering to our neighbours and wish we could have some too, but our parents were always behind with the payments. We were never washed or given clean clothes, so that when my brother and sister and I left the house to go to school we felt ashamed of our dirty clothes and grubby faces. The other kids used to call us the 'smelly Pontings' and we knew that we were the lowest of the low.

Worse than all of this was the abuse we suffered from our father. He was physically violent, beating all of us and humiliating and torturing us in all kinds of ways, such as forcing us to stand naked on a chair for hours as a punishment for the slightest misdemeanour. But he saved his worst torments for the nights, when he would creep into our bedroom and sexually molest me, and later on my younger sister Kim as well.

Those night-time visits were torture. I coped by trying to leave my body and go somewhere else, so that I could disconnect from the small girl whose father was leering over her with his filthy breath, spewing spittle over her and shoving his nicotine-stained fingers inside her. There was no way to escape him. He would pull me into his bed in the mornings to 'play' or trap me in the lounge when Mum was out and I had no choice. He did as he wanted with me and I was little more than an object to him.

Our only saviour from this relentlessly awful existence was a small, round red-haired woman we called Auntie. Margaret Hinton was actually our mother's aunt – our great-aunt – and she lived about half an hour's bus journey from us, in Laycock Mansions, a large pre-war block of flats behind Highbury Corner in Islington.

Every now and then, sometimes for a day or two, at other times for as much as a couple of weeks, Dad would instruct Mum to take us over to 'that old bag' as he called her. Mum would obediently trot us off to the bus stop and deliver us to Auntie who, despite the lack of notice, was always ready to envelop us in her warm hug. Smothered against her generous bosom we breathed in her familiar soap-and-lavender smell and knew that, for the moment, we were safe.

Dad hated Auntie, who had brought Mum up after her own mother died in childbirth. Auntie had seen through him from the start when, as a smooth-talking spiv of twenty-four's he had pursued her pretty nineteen-year-old niece and persuaded her to marry him within days of their meeting. He also persuaded her to hack off her long red hair and swap her contact lenses for thick, ugly glasses. She had been fancied by lots of the young men in the factory where they both worked, and our father didn't want any competition. What Mum ever saw in him, none of us, including Auntie, ever knew. My own guess is that Mum suffered to some extent from learning difficulties and Dad was able to exploit and control her.

The reason he made Mum take us over to Auntie was because he didn't want us around. As soon as he'd claimed all the benefits he could, he spent the money on himself and sent us to Auntie to be clothed and fed. This was especially true as the beginning of each term approached, when Auntie would be the one who bought our new school uniforms and shoes and made sure we were prepared.

Auntie's beloved husband Sid had been killed soon after the war when one of the unexploded bombs that littered London blew up. Auntie and Sid had been unable to have children of their own, so they had doted on our mother, and in due course Auntie doted on me, Kim and Laurence. Dad knew this and used it to get money out of her, threatening that she would never see us again if she failed to 'lend' him and Mum cash that would without doubt never be repaid.

At the time we knew nothing of this: we just loved our time with Auntie and wished with all our hearts that we could live with her always. Her flat was as clean as a pin – she even washed down the communal stairs outside it. The minute we arrived, filthy, hungry and desperate, she would feed us, put us in the bath and scrub off all the dirt and then launder all our clothes. From then on we were warm, well-fed, clean and loved – until out of the blue Mum would turn up to take us back and, reluctantly, we had to kiss Auntie goodbye.

Any happy childhood memories we had were of Auntie and our times with her. We had wonderful outings: picnics in the park, bus rides through London, visits to big, smart shops or strolls through Chapel Street Market while eating huge Italian ice creams. And at the end of each day we would eat one of her delicious dinners and help her wash up before curling up in front of the television to watch *Billy Cotton's Bandstand* or *The Andy Williams Show*. Then Auntie would make us say our prayers – mine was always to be able to stay with her for ever – before tucking us into her big, cosy bed and singing to us, in her high, sweet voice.

It was at Auntie's that I got to know Elsie. She lived a few doors away and would often sit out on her balcony and wave to us.

Elsie was probably only in her mid-thirties, though I thought her much older at the time. She had a round figure and, like Auntie, always wore a nylon overall to protect her clothes while she did her cooking and housework. Elsie's flat, like Auntie's, had just one bedroom. When we were visiting, Auntie would put us in her bed and sleep in the living room, and in Elsie's flat Elsie and her husband George had the bedroom and their son Brian, who was a couple of years younger than me, slept in the living room.

Elsie was a great storyteller and the children in the flats often gathered round to hear her tales. She told us about her time during the war, when she had been evacuated to the countryside to escape from Hitler's bombs. At the end of the story, Elsie would dip her hand into the large pocket of her overall and pull out sweets for all of us children. We were never allowed to stay later than 4.30 p.m. as then she would hurry inside to make dinner for her husband George. He was a portly man who wore spectacles with small round lenses and a grey striped suit. He worked in an office at the local town hall and arrived home at exactly the same time every evening, when Elsie would have his meal ready on the table. We all avoided George, for while Elsie was warm-hearted and kind, with a ready smile, George was bad-tempered and brusque and would as soon cuff one of us out of the way as smile at us.

Over the years I got to know Elsie well. When I reached my teens I would sometimes go over on my own to have a cup of tea with her and she'd tell me stories about her life, or we'd sit and chat about anything from the weather to my school work and my hopes for the future. She was good friends with Auntie, who would smile and wave at us from time to time from her own balcony, half a block away.

When I was fifteen Auntie became ill. By then I had met John Falconer, my first boyfriend, and because I was spending most of my time with him I had seen less of Auntie. I had taken him to meet her, of course, and she had thought him wonderful, but I hadn't stayed over with her for a while because I often stayed at John's home with him and his parents and sisters. On the few occasions when I did, I noticed that Auntie was far more tired than she used to be. It was my older brother Laurence, who was by this time living with Auntie because she was nearer to his school, who told me that she was beginning to do and say odd things. He told me that she was often still in her dressing gown when he got home from school – something that Auntie, who prided herself on her five a.m. start each day and her immaculate clothes and perfectly done hair, would never previously have dreamed of doing. Not only that but she was doing things like peeling the potatoes and then throwing them away and boiling the skins. Concerned, I went over to her flat with Laurence and I could see straight away that a change had taken place. Auntie was muddled and confused. After she went to bed early, Laurence and I talked, but we had no idea what was wrong. All we could do was hope that she would get better and agree to keep a close eye on her.

Two days later Laurence found her on the floor, lying in a pool of blood. She must have fallen and hit her head on the bedpost. She was taken to hospital where she needed stitches and was kept in overnight. It was there that a doctor explained to us that Auntie had developed senile dementia. He explained that little blood vessels in her brain were bursting, causing her to be confused and disorientated. There was no cure, he said, and she would only get worse. He added that she was taking up a bed in his surgical ward and would have to be discharged. So we got Auntie dressed and took her home on the bus.

The three of us – Laurence, Kim and I – nursed Auntie at home for the next few weeks. We knew nothing about social services nor any kind of help that might be on offer. All we knew was that our beloved Auntie was ill and needed us. We did shifts, sleeping beside her and watching her through the day, the three of us – and often my boyfriend John too – sleeping in the living room when we weren't watching her.

It was a tough time. Mostly Auntie didn't know us, but sometimes she would suddenly recognise us and ask what we were doing and why we weren't at school or work. We'd say it was a day off and she'd nod and smile, and soon she would slip away again, back into confusion. We did all we could to remind her of her old life, giving her tea in her special china cup and splashing her favourite lavender water on her. But nothing made any difference.

During this time Elsie was a real friend to us, coming over to ask how Auntie was and bringing us little gifts of food. And sometimes I would take a little break and go and have a cup of tea with Elsie.

Eventually Auntie's two sisters came along and declared that we couldn't look after her and she should be in hospital. They had never been fond of us, considering us to be a burden on her, and although we were distraught we had no say in the matter. We hated the thought of Auntie in a hospital, with no one who loved her to watch over her. But all we could do was kiss her goodbye and watch as Auntie was taken away in an ambulance and her things were packed up and moved out so that the flat could be handed back to the council. It all happened very fast and, unable to watch any more, I went over to Elsie's where she comforted me with a cup of tea.

It was a damp miserable day, and as we sipped our tea we both leaned on the balcony, watching the children below as they played. Elsie asked me how things were going with my boyfriend John. I told her how happy we were and that I hoped one day he would be my husband. I asked her how she had met George.

'I worked with your Auntie as a presser in the clothing factory and we became good friends, although she was older than me. George was a foreman there in them days and, goodness me, he was a looker. You might not think so now, but at the time, he bowled me over.'

I had never considered sour-faced George to be a

good-looking man and tried hard, without much success, to imagine him bowling Elsie over with his looks
and charm.

'Your Auntie was married to Sid and we would
sometimes go out in a foursome. We married and, not
long after, we moved in here.'

Elsie drew in her breath and hesitated before speaking again. 'There is something you should know about
marriage, Jenny. It isn't always easy. I took my vows to
love, honour and obey my husband and I meant it. But
I didn't have any idea what it would mean. As far as
George is concerned I must obey him, even when he
wants things that, well, I don't feel right doing. He's a
powerful man, George, and if I don't do what he says
he's got a strong left hook.'

I was startled. Did Elsie mean that he hit her? And
what 'things' did he make her do? I looked at her,
unsure whether to ask. But there was no need.

'I was pure when I married,' she said. 'I'd never been
near any man and I didn't know what to expect. When
we did the business – you know, sex – on our wedding
night, well, it was awful. George was very rough and I
was shocked at what I had to do to please him. I don't
mean just lying there, I mean things I'd never heard of
that seemed to me very wrong and that made me feel
queasy. He made me have sex in the back passage –
you know, anal – and it hurt so badly. I spent most of
the next day in tears. That was how it began and that
was how it went on. Every night since then I've

dreaded it. George's demands got worse and worse. Not just the anal sex, which was bad enough, but slapping me about as well. And if I didn't do as he wanted he would make me, with his fists.

'I don't know why I'm telling you this now – I never told a soul before. I suppose I just want you to be careful, to make sure you've got the right man, a man who'll be gentle with you, and understanding.

'There were times I wanted to mention it to your Auntie Margaret, but I never did. We just didn't talk of such things. I did try once to talk to my old Mam, but she just told me that women have to bear these things and that it was all part of being a married woman. But I didn't know if that was true – I couldn't believe that all women had to do what I did and get hit if they tried to refuse.

'I know now that they don't. Some women enjoy marital relations, because their husbands are kind and make them feel special. They don't have to be treated like dirt, get hit or do disgusting things.'

Elsie seemed to wander off to some place in her mind and I could see the tears in her eyes. 'I blame myself for our Brian. It was one of those nights when George wanted, you know, S-E-X,' Elsie spelled it out in a whisper, 'and as usual I hated the idea of it. For once I decided to ask him not to do it. He was enraged and told me to get ready for him. I was crying but he didn't pay any attention – he just threw me on the bed and then had his way, so brutally that I was in terrible pain.

'The next morning as I cooked his breakfast he
warned me never to behave that way again and told
me that I was to give myself willingly every time he
wanted "you know what". Nine months later Brian
was born. I looked at him and loved him from the start
– the way he was conceived wasn't his fault. But he was
born with a club foot and George blamed me. He said
that any child born from rape would be handicapped
and if I'd only done my duty willingly Brian would
never have had his bad foot.

'I've carried the guilt with me ever since. I look at the
special boot Brian has to wear and I feel so terrible.'

'You don't really believe that, do you, Elsie?' I said,
incredulous. Even at fifteen I knew that a handicap
couldn't be caused by rape. 'Brian's foot isn't your
fault at all, it's just one of those things that happens.
And even if it was true it would be George's fault, not
yours. He's the one who attacked you.'

'The doctors did explain that it was nothing either of
us had done,' said Elsie. 'But George kept insisting it
was my fault and it's stuck with me. I'd do anything to
help Brian. George isn't kind to him, he shoves him out
of the way and pays no attention to him. But I love him
and I do my best to make him feel special. When he
gets teased, or feels down because he can't play foot-
ball with the other lads, I tell him he's special, chosen
by the angels for a special job in life. And he's doing
well at school – I'm very proud of him. Mind you,
those drums of his drive me crazy. He can't play them

when George is home but he's at them every minute that he can manage. He wants to be in a pop band, and his handicap shouldn't stop him. He's a brave one, is Brian. I'm sure he'll make it.'

Elsie wiped the tears from her eyes. 'You'd best get back to your Auntie's things,' she said. I knew then that Elsie could speak no more. I kissed her goodbye and promised to pop by to see her when I could.

Neither of us knew then that it would be years before I saw Elsie again. Auntie died only a few weeks later and Laurence, Kim and I were grief-stricken. I was so upset that I couldn't bring myself to attend her funeral and I walked around in a daze for weeks, thinking that I saw her on the street or on buses, feeling certain that she couldn't really be dead.

I thought of Elsie often, but I couldn't bring myself to visit the flats, with their memories of Auntie and all the happiness we'd had there. It was one day, about fifteen years later, while I was shopping at the market near the Angel Islington, that I bumped into Brian. He looked incredibly well and very handsome. We chatted and he told me that he was married, with a little girl, and was a successful musician, playing in his own band and as a session musician for some big names.

I asked him for news of Elsie and he told me that she was living in a new flat nearby and gave me the address. A week later I went to visit her. Elsie, now in her fifties, looked well and was delighted to see me. I took my daughter Martine along and Elsie told me all about her granddaughter Lily, who was a little younger than Martine.

Elsie's life had changed when George, who was quite a bit older than her, had died suddenly of a heart attack. 'It was a terrible shock,' she told me. 'I would never have left him, despite what he did to me, because that's how I was brought up. But when he died I was freed from all the pain and humiliation of what he did. I was able to devote myself to Brian, giving him the best life I could and encouraging his music. And a couple of years after Brian left home I met Joe. He was a chap I'd seen for years – he worked on the buses round where I lived and he always gave me a wink when I was on his bus. One day he asked me if I'd like to go out for a drink with him and I said yes. Blushed like a beetroot and couldn't believe I'd done it! We got on like a house on fire and it wasn't long before we were seeing each other all the time.

'When Joe asked me to marry him I didn't hesitate, I knew by then that he was a very different man to George and I wasn't wrong. Joe and me are very happy: it's been eight years now and I never made a better move than marrying him. He's so considerate and kind – he brings me flowers every week and treats me like a lady. And in the bedroom department, well, Joe is a gentleman and he's shown me that it can be wonderful. I'm a very lucky woman.'

I was thrilled to see Elsie glowing with happiness: she deserved it after all she'd put up with through her years with George. Elsie was old school, the kind of woman who gritted her teeth and endured regular abuse, patiently and in silence.

I like to think that today no woman feels she has to do that. Elsie was isolated, but today women talk to one another more about what's really going on, there's support available and it's possible – though not necessarily easy – to walk away from a bad situation and make a fresh start. Elsie's story taught me that things really have improved in many ways and that no woman need tolerate the intolerable.

8
Sonny

I have been privileged to meet some amazing people, and one of the most extraordinary has to be Sonny. I met him during a bleak and horribly unhappy period of my life when I often felt there was very little to live for. Sonny, with his warmth, humour and sense of fun, was always able to cheer me up and he became a very special friend.

When Sonny and I first met I was trying to escape from my daughter's father, a cruel and abusive man. Keith had seemed wonderful when I first met him. He was good-looking, confident and popular and he made me feel special. I didn't see the warning signs that might have told someone older or more experienced to steer clear of him – I was a teenager and very innocent. By the time I realised that Keith could be cruel and sadistic I was expecting our daughter and I felt I had to try to make the relationship work.

For a long time I tried in every way I could. Time after time I forgave Keith for hurting and humiliating me, praying that he'd change. When I realised he never would, I couldn't break free. Changing locks or phone numbers was useless. So was moving house – he was cunning and manipulative and always tracked me down. Each time he did he attacked me, injuring me so badly that several times I ended up in hospital, cut, bruised and with burns and broken bones. Even the law couldn't help me – in those days the police considered Keith's abuse to be a 'domestic' incident and for years they refused to act. It wasn't until Keith kidnapped another woman that the police were able to do anything to stop him.

It was during this time, on a rare night out in London with my girlfriends, that I met Sonny. My friends and I ended up looking for a late-night drink in Covent Garden and as we made our way across the cobbled stones of the market square a gang of youths began shouting abuse at a lone figure who was walking along trying to ignore them.

As the gang's shouts got louder, the man they were targeting came across to our group and asked whether he could join us. With his cropped blond hair, dark blue eyeliner and very tight jeans, it was obvious to all of us that this extremely good-looking young man was gay. We told him that of course he could join us.

He told us his name was Sonny and we invited him to join us for a drink. From the start Sonny and I hit it off and at the end of the evening we exchanged phone numbers.

Sonny turned out to be a wonderful, supportive person. I've spent many great evenings with him and class him as one of my best friends. He's always been there for me. When times were bad, I felt I could call him and talk freely and openly. He would never make a judgement about me or my situation; he'd just be there, listening at the end of the phone.

Sonny was frank about being gay and was very much out of the closet. He was always open and honest about his sexuality and I loved him for it. And perhaps because of that I found that I could talk more freely about sex with Sonny than with some of my female friends. He seemed to be able to understand me so well.

When I think of Sonny I smile – it's rare to meet such a sweet soul. Yet Sonny has had more than his share of difficulties. From the start Sonny felt different from other people. He knew early on that he was gay and that most of the people around him – his parents included – wouldn't find it easy to accept.

Eventually, after realising that he would never feel he belonged in his home town, Sonny made a fresh start in London – which was where we met. He'd already faced a lot of prejudice and criticism, and had dealt with it bravely, so he deserved a few blessings in life. But in London he was to go through an ordeal which left him on the verge of a breakdown.

I met Sonny some time after this traumatic period in his life and had known him for a while before he told me what had happened to him at the hands of a gang of ruthless men. I was amazed that he had survived it with all his natural sweetness intact and without a hint of bitterness.

That's why I want to pass on Sonny's story. Because Sonny found a way through the pain, humiliation and anger he felt after he was attacked, and emerged stronger and wiser. He was able to find the positive, even in such a terrible ordeal, and use it to learn and grow, rather than shrink away from the world.

On the evening when Sonny told me his story Keith had appeared and threatened me. I was upset and scared; I didn't know whether Keith would come back or what to do. I called Sonny and he insisted that we go out for a drink and talk. I was only too eager to get away from my flat, so, leaving Martine with a friend, I set out to meet Sonny in a local pub.

When I got there Sonny gave me a hug and we sat at a table close to the roaring fire. Easy-listening music was playing in the background and it was cosy and intimate, the perfect setting for me to begin to unwind. I began pouring out my troubles and I remember thinking that I was the only one in the world that had problems. When I'd finished telling him about Keith's threats and attacks, Sonny said that he too had experienced a nightmare in his life.

It was my turn to listen. Sonny and I had developed real trust between us and he obviously felt ready to talk about what had happened to him. His was a shocking account and it can't have been easy for him to talk about it. But I was glad that he did –

and not only about what he had been through but also about his journey back to health and sanity.

Sonny began by telling me a little about his child-hood. 'I remember growing up in Bradford, and think-ing – no – *knowing* that I was different from other boys,' he said. Then he began to tell me his harrowing story.

My parents could see it, but Mum never said a word and Dad coped by ignoring me. He came from a very macho background: in his world men didn't talk about feelings, they spent their waking hours at work or in the pub, and as far as they were concerned women were there to look after the home and put meals on the table. So it must have been a big deal for Dad that his son was gay. He only ever made reference to it once and that was to thump me and call me a bloody poof. I hoped he would come to terms with it and accept me, but our relationship never changed and he went to his grave ashamed of me.

I wasn't sure how Mum felt, but after Dad died she seemed to be more relaxed about it and now she accepts that I'm gay and is proud that I've done so well.

But at that time, back before Dad died, I felt I couldn't stay in Bradford. I wanted to train as a stylist and I decided to move to London in the hope that I'd find acceptance and be able to fit in.

When I first arrived I was so excited. I found all the

gay clubs and soon made lots of friends. Times were hard, though, and my career in styling was slow to take off. After a few months my money had run out and I was finding it hard to survive. Mum had bailed me out a few times, but I just couldn't make ends meet and I didn't want to ask her for money again. I had to prove to myself that I could make it on my own.

One night, with just a couple of pounds in my pocket, I made my way to a well-known gay haunt. I sat at the bar, nursing my bottle of beer and wondering what to do next. An older man in a dark suit approached me and we started to chat. He seemed a nice guy, but when he asked me to go back to his flat for a drink I hesitated. He saw my doubts and assured me that there wouldn't be any funny business. He said he just wanted company and to have a chat.

He appeared to be true to his word. When we got to his flat he offered me a drink and invited me to sit down, without making any kind of move on me. Before long I had poured out my story and he listened intently. He said he knew some people in the fashion world and would ask around to see if he could fix me up with a few interviews. I was over the moon. We made arrangements to meet again in the same bar a few days later.

I was excited at the prospect of a possible job and couldn't wait to meet him again. He arrived as promised and gave me a piece of paper with the name and address of a contact of his who, he said, would be interested in seeing me for a possible assistant stylist's job in a couple of days' time. I almost skipped home that evening, already planning what to wear for my interview and what I would say to impress my prospective employer. The meeting had been set up in Whitechapel. I knew the area well as it was one of the centres of the fashion industry and I'd been for several job interviews there.

It was early evening when I made my way to the address I'd been given, a studio apartment in a former warehouse. Nervous and excited, I rang the bell. A man's voice told me to take the lift to the penthouse flat. As I entered the large open-plan apartment I saw that there were four men there. They were all busy, two looking at photos and the other two chatting together over a magazine spread that lay on a low table in front of them. One of these two men got up and came over to me. He held out his hand to shake mine and introduced himself as Rob.

I could see instantly that Rob was high on drugs. His speech was slightly slurred, he looked pale and a little sweaty and his eyes were darting from side to side. I was sure he'd been taking cocaine, but it didn't shock me. In fact, I wasn't even surprised: I had already learned that in some parts of the fashion industry everyone was on something. I looked around the room and noticed empty beer bottles and half-empty bottles of vodka and Scotch strewn everywhere. It looked as if I'd come to a party rather than an interview.

As I stood there, the other man at the table spoke. 'So you're the entertainment for tonight,' he drawled, without even looking up at me. I apologised and said that he must have been mistaken because I was there for a job interview. He looked up. 'That's what George tells all of them,' he said. 'Now stop fucking acting the innocent and get your clothes off.' Alarmed, I said that I had better leave, as I was genuinely there for a job and there must have been a mistake. I turned and made my way to the lift.

Rob moved rapidly across the room and put his arm in front of me. 'Where do you think you're going, pretty boy?' he said, his eyes rolling about even more crazily. I pushed him out of the way. I was getting scared now. I'd understood that this was a set-up and I realised that I needed to get away, and fast. But the four men were too quick for me and too strong. In what seemed like seconds I was pinned down on the floor, with one guy on my back, weighing me down, while the others started to strip me. All I could hear was someone muttering 'Fucking poof' and their drug-fuelled laughter.

'Let's give him a little something to calm him down,' I heard one of the men say. I was rolled over onto my back and then one of them grabbed my head and tilted it back. Powder was poured into my nose. It was cocaine, I knew instantly. The taste as the powder hit the back of my throat was vile. I must have pulled a face, and as I did, they opened my mouth and poured neat vodka down my throat. It was only as I began to choke that they propped me up into a sitting position.

Naked and dazed, I looked at them. Their faces were a blur and even now I can only remember Rob. The other three are faceless in my memory. My head was pulled down and I was forced to give oral sex to one of them, but I don't know who it was. When he'd had enough I was made to do it again and again to the others. After a while I felt more powder poured up my nose and more drink forced into my mouth.

To be honest, Jen, once the drink and drugs hit me I was off my head. But I'm glad in a way, because it helped me to shut out some of what followed.

To those men I was no more than an object, to be used as and when they wanted. They all raped me. I remember the pain and I remember the laughter as each one took his turn. In the end I was so numb with shock and the drink and drugs that I just wanted to sleep and wake up somewhere else and be safe again.

And that was exactly what happened. I must have blacked out and when I woke up I was sprawled in a shop doorway. I was partially dressed, with my pants and jeans on, and the rest of my belongings were next to me. I can remember breathing out and seeing my breath form a mist from the chill in the air. I looked at my watch, and it said six-fifteen a.m. I had gone for the interview at eight p.m. the previous evening.

I remember finding a phone box and calling a cab to take me home. I don't remember paying the driver or getting inside my little flat, I just remember thinking I had been lucky to have been dumped somewhere and not killed. I was so relieved, but in pain and utterly shocked and humiliated. I fell on the bed and slept for hours.

It wasn't easy coping afterwards. I stayed in the flat for a couple of days, just sleeping. I burned the clothes that I'd been wearing and I cried a lot. I felt I'd been such a fool not to have understood that I was being set up and I kept thinking about my attackers just laughing at me. I thought about going back to Bradford, or giving up my dream of becoming a stylist. But I decided to stay in London and stick it out. I wanted to prove to those men – and to anyone who'd ever doubted me – that I could make it.

I pulled myself together and went on looking for a job and at first I felt I was coping pretty well. But when I was offered an interview a couple of weeks later, I set off from home and broke down halfway there. I started shaking, thinking of the last 'interview' I'd been to. I was sitting on the Tube and I started to sob – I just couldn't stop myself. I was conscious of everyone looking at me but I couldn't control the tears, so I got off and sat on a bench on the platform, trying to calm down. I realised that I couldn't face going to the interview, but I couldn't face getting myself home either and I didn't know what to do.

That was when I met an angel – well, I call him that. Jamie was a young guy who saw the state I was in and came and sat down beside me. He offered me a hanky and asked if he could buy me a cup of tea. Shakily I agreed, and he led me up the escalator and out to a café next to the station. After a cup of strong tea I felt calmer and stopped crying. I apologised, but Jamie just smiled and said, 'that's fine, mate, you look as though you've had a tough time.' I told him that I had and, without going into the whole story, I explained that I'd been assaulted only a couple of weeks earlier.

Jamie got out a piece of paper and a pen and scribbled something down. Then he handed it to me and said, 'These people are good. If you need someone to talk to, try them.' He explained that he'd seen a counsellor recently for a problem of his own, and that it had really helped. Then, with a cheery goodbye, he paid for the tea, wished me well and left.

That moment of kindness from a stranger made all the difference to me. Just knowing that someone cared, and had helped me without expecting anything from me in return, gave me back a tiny bit of trust in the world. I looked at the card, which had the name of an organisation and a phone number on it. I didn't know what the organisation was but I felt I had nothing to lose, so I went home and called them.

It turned out to be a gay support organisation and I was told that I could see a counsellor there for free the following week. I'd never thought about counselling, but I knew that I needed help so I went along.

I was terribly nervous, but the counsellor, a middle-aged man, put me at ease and just let me talk. I told him the whole story and he listened sympathetically. He didn't judge or look shocked or try to comfort me – he was just *there* for me.

I saw the counsellor once a week for the next six months and it was a real lifeline. That regular appointment got me through each seven-day spell and as the months went by I began to feel stronger and more in charge of my life than I ever had before.

The counsellor helped me to work through what had happened. At the same time he showed me how to keep it in perspective and not allow it to ruin my life. He also helped me to stop blaming myself for being tricked. After all, it could have happened to anyone.

By the end of the six months I was back on my feet. The counsellor had given me the support I needed and at the same time helped me to see that I was actually a strong person who could cope with an awful lot. Most important of all, the whole affair showed me that I would always have a choice about how I dealt with any situation. In the case of the attack, I could either let it ruin my life or I could choose to learn from it and move on.

Soon after I finished the counselling I got my first job, as an assistant stylist. I was so happy that I threw myself into it, putting in long hours and learning everything I could. I loved the business and I did well, working my way up and learning from top people.

*   *   *

I asked Sonny about the man he had met originally. The one who had offered to help and had sent him off to the 'interview', setting him up to be attacked.

Sonny nodded. 'I was coming to him, because you're right, there's another piece of the story missing. At first I did look for him. I imagined myself screaming at him that I'd tell the police what he'd done. But as the weeks passed and there was no sign of him, I gave up.

'Then, about a year later, I saw him again, in a bar. He was hitting on another young boy. I approached him with my heart in my mouth. Time had passed and I'd had the counselling, so I had no intention of screaming or threatening him. I wanted to do something far more important – it was my chance to save another boy from the same awful ordeal. I ignored George and talked to the boy, warning him not to trust the man. The boy scurried off and I was thrilled. George didn't seem worried – he just strolled off – but I didn't care: I had helped someone else to avoid what had happened to me. I think that was another big step in my recovery: I realised that I had the power to do something good for someone else, and that made me feel so happy.'

I asked Sonny why he hadn't reported what had happened to the police.

'At the time I didn't even consider it,' he said. 'I felt such a fool, I was sure they'd just think I was another silly young boy who'd got involved in some drink-and-drugs scene.

'Later, when I felt stronger, I wished I had told the cops. So when I saw George up to his tricks again I did go to the police. I told them that he was preying on young men and gave them his description and they took me seriously. But they explained that it would be difficult to prove anything against him – after all, he was just offering young men job interviews. They needed to catch the people at the other end of the set-up as well, and link them to George. I never heard any more about it, so I don't suppose they got him, or the other men. But at least I did the right thing.'

Sonny smiled. 'I was lucky, Jen. I met the "angel" on the Tube, and then the counsellor, and then I got a great job. I was given chances and I grabbed them, and that's what got me through.'

Sonny had a lot to be proud of. Five years on he was a top stylist, getting celebrities ready for magazine photo shoots and with a waiting list of people who wanted him to work for them. And he thoroughly deserved his success: he'd worked incredibly hard and he'd found the courage to put his ordeal behind him.

'I could have spent the rest of my life feeling like dirt,' he told me. 'But I wasn't going to give the men who had hurt me that much power over me. Why should I let them ruin my life? I'd rather show them that they don't matter at all to me, that they're vermin. Let them ruin their own lives – no one who does what they did can feel good about themselves inside. But my life is for me, and I'm going to live it and be happy.'

I learned a lot from Sonny that night – about surviving, about being strong and about making a decision not to let evil people ruin your life.

After our talk I watched him walk to the bar, confident and with his head held high. As he reached the counter he turned and grinned at me. 'I think I'll make it a large one, babe,' he said – and winked.

I smiled. That was Sonny: brave, bright and funny, no matter what. I was proud to be his friend and I felt that in trusting each other with our most painful stories our friendship had grown deeper and stronger.

9
Margaret

Margaret's story highlights one of the most secret and silent kinds of abuse. Incest is still so taboo that it's seldom spoken of. Most people would rather think that it just doesn't happen. But, sadly, it does, and in many seemingly ordinary and normal families too. Incest doesn't just happen between fathers and daughters: it can occur between any two family members and, as Margaret's story shows, sometimes between a brother and sister.

Margaret and I first met many years ago when a mutual friend brought her down to the pub I owned for a quick drink. We got on instantly and after that the three of us would often go out together for girls' nights out. Margaret was in her late twenties, very petite and pretty, with thick dark curly hair that tumbled down her back. She had a lovely oval face and a nice smile. But her personality didn't match her angelic appearance. When I first met her I expected her to be shy and quiet, but she was the total opposite. She could drink a pint of lager faster than any man I knew, crack obscene jokes and swear like a trooper – even in mixed company – and hold her own in any argument. Margaret was a real little bombshell.

On one of our nights out we all decided to go back to the pub for a nightcap. We propped up the bar and chatted for hours, putting the world to rights and laughing and joking about anything and everything. We were all eventually the worse for wear and our friend decided it was time for some black coffee. Then she disappeared off home. Margaret and I decided to have one more quick drink before we went to bed.

As I went round to the other side of the bar to get two more vodkas Margaret suddenly asked me how many brothers I had, and if I loved them. Surprised, I replied that I'd had two, and loved them both very much.

I told her that my younger brother Chris had died, at the age of seventeen, after sniffing glue. That had been some years earlier, but I still thought about him every day and missed him. He had been seven years younger than me and he and our younger sister Carole had been left at home with our abusive, violent father and neglectful, cowed mother after we three older ones had left home. Living with a father who tormented him every day of his life had been too much for Chris, who was a gentle and loving soul, and for the last couple of years of his life he'd found his escape in a bag of glue.

My other brother Laurence, who was a year older than me, was always there for me and the others when we were children and were struggling to survive life without proper food, warmth or care and in constant fear of our father. Laurence saw his role as the protector of the rest of us and did his best to stop Dad hurting us. He even took the blame for things one of us had done, knowing it would mean taking the vicious beating that always followed. And when he was thirteen and Dad was beating Mum up yet again he waded in, trying to stop Dad, and ended up in hospital with a broken nose.

I smiled. 'Dad never touched him again, though. He was a brave boy. And even after we grew up and left home, Laurence helped me out several times with money or a place to live. It was always good to know that I had a big brother looking out for me.'

Puzzled that Margaret's question had come out of the blue, I asked her why she had wanted to know.

Margaret sighed. 'I knew you had a rough time as a kid, Jen, but I wish I'd had an older brother like yours. I've got three brothers, but I don't talk to the oldest at all.'

Curious, I asked why.

After a long pause, Margaret, her eyes fixed on the bar in front of her, replied. 'My brother assaulted and raped me for seven years.'

I was both shocked and horrified. My brother would never have done such a thing, but my father had and I certainly understood the sense of horror that Margaret must have felt at being hurt and abused by someone who should have loved and cared for her.

I asked whether she would like to tell me about it, and she nodded. I slipped onto the stool beside hers and we sipped our drinks as she talked. This is what Margaret told me.

It all started as a game. Ronnie was six years older than me, the oldest of us kids. He would often come and play with me and our little sister Lorraine in our room, when our two other brothers were busy with a game of their own. One night when Lorraine had fallen asleep, he asked me to play a different game. He wanted me to play with his willy.

I was just a kid at the time, only eight years old, and I thought it was funny. But Ronnie was nearly fourteen and I realise now that he knew just what he was doing. He called it his game of doctors and nurses. I was pleased that he wanted to play a special game with me on my own – it made me feel grown-up. So I agreed and did as he asked. He wanted me to rub his willy, which I thought was pretty silly. I was surprised, though, when it went all big and hard – I'd had no idea that a willy could do that. I asked him about it but he said to keep quiet, that it meant I was special and that we shouldn't tell the others or Mum and Dad about our game.

After that night I forgot about it, until a few weeks later Ronnie asked me to play it again. I didn't really want to, but I didn't like to say no, so I agreed. The same thing happened, and when his willy went hard he asked me to rub it even harder and his face started to go pink. I thought it was weird.

Over the next few years we played the game a few more times. It wasn't often, and looking back I can see that this was probably because Ronnie didn't get many opportunities to get me alone – I shared a room with Lorraine and he shared with our other brothers. In any case, he was busy with his friends and school work, he just played the willy game when there was nothing else going on and no one around.

Time passed and I was a quick developer. By the time I was twelve I had boobs and could easily pass for a few years older. Ronnie must have noticed this and decided it was time for some more grown-up games. He was now about eighteen and very handsome. He'd left school by this time and was working. He was very popular with his crowd of friends and he had a girlfriend, so I don't know why he needed to abuse me – I'm sure he could have had sex elsewhere if he'd wanted it. But Ronnie preferred to play games with his little sister. Perhaps he liked the idea of dominating me and of being in control. It was almost as if he loved the fact that he had got to me first. He would always tell me how very special I was.

At any rate, when everyone else was asleep, or out, he would come into the room and play with my private parts under the sheets, while masturbating himself at the same time. I felt a bit uncomfortable about it and didn't really enjoy it. But I had always looked up to Ronnie so it just didn't occur to me that what he was doing was wrong, or that I could say no.

On the first night that he raped me I was in bed with a nasty cold. Mum and Dad and the others had gone to watch Lorraine in her school play, but Ronnie had offered to stay at home and look after me. I can still see him popping his head around the bedroom door and asking me if I wanted a cuppa. I said yes, and within minutes he was back with a hot cup of tea.

As he placed the tea on the bedroom chest of drawers Ronnie slipped his hand under the covers and began fondling me. He told me to do exactly as he said, and whispered that he had something very special for me that night. Then he stripped, climbed into the bed with me and raped me. Afterwards he held me close and told me how much he loved me and that I was his special girl, more special than his girlfriend, but I wasn't to tell anyone as they wouldn't understand.

I told him that I loved him too, and would do anything he asked me. What he'd done to me had hurt, but I knew that Ronnie liked it and I told myself it was OK because he was my brother and cared about me. And that was important. Our parents weren't cruel, but they were never warm with us – they didn't give us kisses and hugs and I never felt loved or special with them. So when I got that from Ronnie I lapped it up. I was a little girl desperate for affection and he filled the gap.

After he had left my room I saw that there was blood on the sheets. I told Ronnie, who said it was OK, that was just my period and not to worry about it. So I took the sheets off and washed them before the others came back.

I got back into bed before Mum and Dad and the others got home. My vagina was hurting, but I knew that I mustn't say anything: it was our secret and Ronnie would say I had spoiled it if I told.

After that Ronnie regularly had sex with me. It was surprising how often he managed to get me alone in the house. And I went along with it. I didn't particularly enjoy what he was doing but I didn't hate it either. It made me feel special, Ronnie's special sister. Every time he had sex with me I bled, but he always told me it didn't matter and I always obediently cleaned the sheets before anyone could notice.

Although I was well-developed physically I was incredibly innocent. I trusted and loved Ronnie and had no idea that what he was doing was illegal and wrong, even though it carried on until I was fifteen. At school when all the girls talked about boyfriends and relationships, sex and love, I smiled to myself, knowing that I had Ronnie. I was so ignorant – I must have been stupid, I simply had no idea that what we were doing was wrong.

One evening, when I was fifteen and Ronnie was twenty-one, everything changed. Ronnie came in and announced to the whole family that he was getting engaged, and that he would be setting up home with his girlfriend. I remember sitting on the sofa, staring at him and thinking that it must be a joke, Ronnie was mine, he had told me he was, so many times, surely no one else was going to come between us. As he stood, coolly telling the family all about his plans, I wanted to explode, and eventually I did. I screamed at him – I don't remember the exact words, but I didn't give the secret away, I just shouted that he couldn't leave us. The rest of the family stared at me, open-mouthed, and I stormed out and went to my room.

Ronnie quickly followed me. He must have told the others that he'd calm me down. I had thrown myself on my bed, sobbing. Ronnie came in and sat next to me. He put his arms round me and held me close. He told me that he couldn't be with me any more, not even secretly and that it was time for him and me to move on. But I was still shocked and didn't understand why. I begged and pleaded with him not to leave and at that point Ronnie got angry. Clasping my face between his hands, he spoke to me through clenched teeth and in a whisper.

He told me that I was a stupid little shit. Didn't I know that a brother and sister having sex with each other was illegal? Didn't I know he could never be with me permanently and legally, and didn't I know that I should be grateful that I had been getting a regular fuck? He released my face and walked to the door. Turning round, he smiled at me. 'Don't bother trying to tell anyone,' he said. 'They'll just think you're a jealous little liar.'

I believed him. Ronnie was the star of the family. He was everything our parents could possibly have wanted from a son. And I was way down in the pecking order. So I never said a thing. When Mum asked me why I was so upset about Ronnie leaving I just said I didn't want the family to break up. But the shock of what Ronnie had said to me that night took a long time to get over. It was only in that moment that I had understood everything – that what he'd done to me was wrong, that he wasn't 'mine' at all but had been using me, and that I had been gullible and naive.

I cried myself to sleep many times, feeling completely alone in the world. Lorraine used to ask me what was wrong, but I fobbed her off and in the end she gave up asking. I felt tainted and dirty, as though I was different from other girls. I was sure that I'd never get a real boyfriend – I thought they'd be able to tell that something was wrong with me. So for a long time I avoided going out with my friends and meeting boys.

Things began to change when I got a Saturday job and met a lovely boy who worked in the same shop. Every week he chatted to me and, although I held back at first, he was so natural and warm that I began to thaw out. When he asked me out I agreed to go, and when he kissed me, on the second date, he told me I was beautiful. That boy, Ted, never knew it, but he did so much to help me heal the wounds. We went out for a year and he made me realise that – on the outside, at least – I wasn't different, I was just like everyone else.

I tried to put what had happened to the back of my mind and get on with my life. I left home, got a good job and found a flat to share with a friend. But every time I saw Ronnie – at family get-togethers – it all came back. He didn't seem bothered: he greeted me and chatted away just as he did with the rest of the family. But I felt all the old hurt and horror come back and I dreaded being around him.

In the end I decided that I wouldn't see him again. The rest of the family couldn't understand it but I just told them that we didn't get on and that was that. I refused to go to family gatherings if Ronnie was there – I saw them all at other times.

I don't know what Ronnie felt about it, he knew why I wouldn't see him and I hope he felt guilty. But what really mattered was what it did for me. The minute I made the decision that he was out of my life I felt a million times better: stronger, braver and in charge of my future. For once *I* was deciding how things would be and it felt good.

That was ten years ago and I've never looked back. I heard that Ronnie's marriage broke up and I felt sorry for his wife and kids, but I wasn't tempted to get in touch with him. These days I do things my way, say what I think and don't take shit from anyone.

Maybe I sound heartless, but I'm doing what I need to do. I know it wouldn't work for everyone, but for me a clean break was the answer. I've developed a tough shell and I'm OK with it – so everyone else just has to put up with it.

Margaret looked up at me and we both laughed. 'Good for you,' I said. 'You've found your own way through and look at you now – you're great-looking, fantastic company and I can't imagine any bloke getting the better of you.'

A few weeks later I saw Margaret again. As usual her spirits were high and she told me that she had a new job. 'I've studied for years and at last I am finally in a position to start teaching,' she said. 'I'll be doing what I've always wanted to do, teaching children with special needs. These kids deserve help and recognition and someone to fight their corner.'

I couldn't think of a better person for those children to have on their side!

10
Judy

It never ceases to amaze me how stories of real suffering often come from the most unlikely people. Judy is a prime example. She's strong and self-willed, articulate and clever, and has a wicked sense of humour. Judy seems fully in control of her life, she knows what she wants and is the very last person you'd ever imagine putting up with cruelty and abuse from anyone.

That was why I was so intrigued when I heard her story. How had Judy made the leap from being, as she describes, a downtrodden wife to the vibrant woman I met? She had clearly turned her life around, and I wanted to know her secret.

Judy is in her early forties. She has two beautiful children and is divorced. She is very open about her failed marriage and what she went through in the years when she was married to her children's father. And, not surprisingly, she has strong opinions about the issue of rape in marriage. Not so long ago it wasn't a crime at all: wives just had to put up with forced sex from their husbands, even when it was violent. But after a new ruling in 2006 it's not only a crime, but a rapist husband can get as long in prison as a stranger who drags a woman into an alley and rapes her. In fact, the law now says that the husband's offence is worse because he is abusing the trust of someone close to him. Judy was jubilant when she heard that, because it gives wives like her the chance to be protected, to fight back and to change what happens to them.

I met Judy through a mutual friend and liked her straight away. Honest and open, she is also friendly and good company. It was on a hen weekend for a friend that Judy told me the story of her marriage. We began talking about the hopes and dreams we'd had for our own marriages, and how much we wanted our friend's marriage to work out. Judy told me her own marriage had gone very wrong, and when I asked her why, she told me her story.

She explained that she had first met her husband fifteen years ago in a nightclub. Stan was quite a bit older than she was and she fell for him on the rebound, after breaking up with her long-term boyfriend.

'Steve had devastated me,' Judy said. 'We'd met when I was nineteen and I thought we'd be together always. But after nearly seven years together he told me that he didn't love me any more and that we should sell the house we'd bought together and go our separate ways. I hadn't seen it coming and couldn't believe it. I was like a lost soul, wandering around for months afterwards, doing anything to help me forget. When I lost Steve I lost most of my friends too. Our friends had mostly been couples, like us, and I soon heard that

Steve was with someone else and our friends had stuck with him and his new girlfriend. A few people still invited me out, but the last thing I wanted was to play gooseberry to a happy couple. So I found myself alone, with no friends and no home, and I had no choice but to go back to my parents.' Judy's story of abuse and fightback really begins at this point.

After a few months I began to feel a bit better, so when my sister Janet suggested a night out I decided to go with her. For the first time in ages, I got myself ready and felt excited about going out. I had missed having a bit of nightlife and couldn't wait to go to the newly refurbished disco in town.

When we got to the club, it was heaving with people and the music was so loud that the club floor seemed to pulsate with the rhythm. The dance floor was packed with people jumping and gyrating to the music and the bar areas were full of thirsty punters, clamouring for drinks.

Janet and I made our way to the bar, jostling and pushing our way through the crowds. Before we even got there, someone stopped me and said, 'Hey, it is you, Judy, isn't it?' I'm only five foot nothing and I really had to look up to see the face of the tall man in front of me. 'Goodness,' I said. 'Is that you, Lee?'

Lee Soper was an old workmate. I hadn't seen him since I'd met Steve, changed jobs and moved to a new area almost eight years earlier. He looked exactly the same, tall and lanky with cropped hair and a wide, welcoming smile. 'I'm here with some friends,' he shouted. I replied that I had only just arrived and hadn't made it to the bar yet, but that once I'd got a drink I'd try to meet up with him to have a chat and catch up on the past eight years.

That wouldn't take long, I thought. What was there to say, really? I'd met Steve, fallen head over heels in love with him, moved job, moved house, wasted seven years of my life and now I had no friends and was back in the cattle market, looking for something – anything – to help me forget.

Janet and I eventually made it to the bar and then made our way through to the edge of the dance floor. I felt a little disheartened at how young some of the people there were. At twenty-seven, I really felt old and out of touch and I was beginning to think that coming to the club hadn't been such a good idea.

Janet must have noticed that I looked uncomfortable because she kept giving me reassuring smiles. She knew that I was thinking about Steve. Everywhere I looked something would trigger off a memory of him, and I wished he was with me. But he wasn't, and I had to move on.

Janet persuaded me to dance and once I was on the dance floor and onto my second drink I started to relax. I felt a tap on my shoulder and turned around to see Lee. 'Hi, Judy' he shouted. 'Fancy a drink?' I nodded and we moved to the edge of the dance floor, where he started to introduce his mates to me. 'This is Wayne, and this is Stan,' he said.

We grabbed a free table and Stan made a point of sitting next to me. And as the evening went on I found myself absorbed in conversation with him. He was witty and entertaining and a good listener, and when he offered to take me home I agreed. Janet wanted to stay on a little longer at the club, so I left her with Lee and Wayne.

As we made our way through the centre of town Stan slipped his hand into mine. For the first time in months I began to feel happy and as I gazed into this man's face I felt a warmth that had been missing inside me for a long time. We reached the place where Stan had parked his car, a gorgeous white BMW soft-top convertible, and I couldn't help but be impressed.

He opened the car door for me and asked what music I would like to hear. We both liked Luther Vandross and so he put some on. It was a warm sultry night and he let the roof down, and as we drove away I felt like a million dollars.

Stan was tall, dark and good-looking and I couldn't believe my luck. He was smartly dressed, seemed to be well off and was twelve years older than me – his dark hair was tinged with white around the ears. I felt he was just what I needed, someone mature and well-balanced.

Within weeks we were seeing each other regularly. As I saw more and more of Stan I thought of Steve less and less. Stan was such a gentleman: he was half Asian and treated me so politely that I always felt special.

We didn't sleep together for several weeks. When we eventually did, although there were no fireworks I thought we'd get used to one another and would become more relaxed with time.

Within three months of meeting Stan, he asked me to marry him. Strangely, when he asked me my heart said no but my head said yes. What I mean is that I wasn't certain whether I was in love with him, but I did think he would be a good husband and that it would be sensible for me to marry him. After all, I wasn't getting any younger, and Stan had a good job and really cared about me. He was offering me safety and security and I felt I'd be a fool to turn all that down. How I wish now that I had listened to my heart, where my doubts lay.

Despite the fact that Stan was half Asian – on his father's side – he had no religious convictions and was happy to go along with my dream of a big white wedding in church. The wedding was set for a few months later, in November, and I was so caught up in all the arrangements that I really didn't have time to think. If I had niggling doubts I didn't allow them to surface. Every time I should have hit the brakes and stopped the process I hit the accelerator instead.

The wedding itself went by in a blur, and after a short honeymoon we moved into a new house. Stan went back to work and I was left at home – I'd left my job when we moved. Stan wanted me to stay at home, but I was soon lonely and bored. I decided to get a job, so that I'd have something to do.

I'd seen an advertisement for a secretarial job with a local estate agent so I applied, without consulting Stan. When I got the job I was thrilled, but Stan was not happy and for the first time in our relationship we argued. I must admit I was shocked by how angry he was. When we went to bed that night we were both still angry and I hoped we could just go to sleep and sort it out in the morning.

But Stan had other ideas. He made it clear that he wanted to have sex, but I refused and pushed his hand away. I needed us to make up first. He became more insistent and I made it clear that I didn't want it – I wasn't in the mood at all. I asked him to leave me alone. Stan only seemed inflamed by my refusal. He pinned me down and forced himself on me, hurting me and ignoring my tears.

After he had finished he rolled over and fell asleep. As he snored, I lay awake, shocked by what he had done. It was as though he'd thought my refusal to have sex was a come-on. I couldn't have made my reluctance more clear, yet he only seemed more determined. This was a side of Stan that I hadn't seen before and I felt afraid. Eventually I quietly cried myself to sleep.

I had hoped that Stan's behaviour was something he would regret and apologise for, but in fact it was the start of how our married life was to be. Every time Stan and I argued, which was more and more often, I would say no to sex and he would force me. I tried everything – I explained to him that I meant it when I said no and I wanted him to leave me alone, but he told me to shut up. I soon realised that Stan believed that if he wanted sex he was entitled to it, no matter what I thought or felt. I had believed that I was marrying a gentleman, but Stan was actually more like a caveman who thought his woman was a possession, to be controlled and used like anything else he owned.

Despite his objections, I had started the job at the estate agent's and I loved it. It was always busy in the agency and I found myself staying late – partly to avoid going home. When I was offered promotion to the post of negotiator I jumped at the chance. But once again Stan was furious and insisted on sex. I think he felt threatened by my growing independence, and forcing himself on me made him feel back in control. But it was a heavy price for me to have to pay.

Once Stan had forced me to have sex a few times I was unable to make love with him willingly again. Any tenderness and warmth I felt for him soon disappeared. His rough demands disgusted me and I began wondering whether to leave him, believing that it was my only way out.

At first I didn't call what Stan was doing to me rape. Although I knew he was wrong to do it, I didn't understand that it *was* rape until I read a magazine article about it. I had thought rape only occurred, when a stranger forced a woman to have sex. So a light went on in my head when I read that a woman could also be raped by her husband.

And it wasn't just the rapes, which were regular and dreadful, leaving me bruised, demoralised and feeling violated. By day things weren't much better. Stan battered away at me verbally, going on and on endlessly about what I must do, my shortcomings and what he wanted.

Looking back I wonder why I didn't walk out straight away. But I dreaded telling my family and friends that it hadn't worked out, especially after all the fuss of the big wedding. All my family adored Stan and they would have been so upset if they'd known I wanted out of the marriage. So I hesitated, burying myself in work, rather than face up to how awful my marriage was.

A couple of months later I was made Employee of the Month at work, earning a nice bonus and a free weekend away. I dreaded having to spend a weekend with Stan and decided not to tell him, but I told my sister and, excited by my success, she told him. It wasn't Janet's fault; as far as the family knew, I was happy with Stan.

We headed off to London for our weekend away. I was pleased because there was lots to do there, and we even managed to book a West End show on the Saturday night. It was a great production and after we returned to the hotel we had a late meal and a couple of bottles of wine.

That night Stan wanted to have sex and, lulled by the wine, I reluctantly agreed. He loved it but I felt very unhappy, knowing that I had only agreed as an alternative to being raped.

A few weeks later I discovered that I was pregnant. Stan was thrilled and Mum and Dad were over the moon at the thought of becoming grandparents, but to me it was like a nail in my coffin. If the thought of leaving Stan had ever entered my head, putting it into action was now impossible. Instead of all the joy most expectant mothers feel I felt totally alone and trapped.

I tried to avoid Stan throughout the pregnancy but, despite my swollen belly, he still insisted on having sex. I gritted my teeth every time: I felt invaded and more and more hopeless.

My job had been my escape, but now Stan insisted that I give up work. I tried to persuade him to let me stay, but he became furiously angry and told me that I was to do as he said, or something would be wrong with the baby. I knew, logically, that this wasn't true, but I felt ground down by him and in the end I just wasn't strong enough to stand up to him. If there had been something wrong with the baby he would have blamed me, and I would have blamed myself too.

After that I think I must have gone into a kind of depression. I was like a robot that did his bidding just to keep the peace. My days were spent preparing for my baby and cooking for Stan. And when my family noticed that I seemed down, they told me it was the pregnancy and that I'd soon feel better.

By the time our son was born, I was a totally different person to the one I had been when I had first met Stan, only two years earlier. Ground down by the night-time assaults and daily verbal batterings I had no sense of self any longer. As Stan stood holding our baby, I felt nothing. Looking back it's clear how mentally drained I must have been, and yet no one, not even me, understood at the time how unwell I was and how much I needed help.

As the months slowly passed, and I didn't improve, my parents and Stan insisted that I should go to the doctor. He diagnosed post-natal depression and gave me antidepressants. To be honest, all they did was make me sleep for hours. Even when I was awake I found myself daydreaming most of the time away in a blur. Thankfully my mum took over the care of the baby.

Stan made full use of my inability to argue or fight back. In my trance-like state I was easy prey for a man who wanted to control me mentally and physically. And, as a result, three months after my son was born I was pregnant again. I was so out of it that I don't remember anything leading up to the pregnancy, or how or when he made me pregnant again. When my daughter was born my state hadn't improved.

Most women say that the birth of a child is one of

the most memorable things that has ever happened to them. I wish I could say that, but I can't. I adore both my son and my daughter, but the pleasure that I should have had from their births was wiped out by their father's cruel behaviour. Stan obviously loved the effect the antidepressants had: far from worrying or expressing concern about my zombie-like state he fed them to me, making sure I took them daily and returned to the doctor for more.

Stan never hit me. The only violence he showed was when he forced sex on me, pinning me down, handling me roughly and snarling that I had to shut up and do as he said. Yet day by day Stan took me to the point where now there are no clear memories, just a large gap in my life. Throughout the first three years of my children's lives I was on drugs that made it hard for me to function, and I had severe periods of depression. And throughout this time, my husband continued to order me about by day and rape me by night – although it must have been like having sex with a dummy.

Throughout the early years of their lives I hadn't been much of a mother to my children. In fact I was dependent on my family – and especially my mother – to help me cope. I felt sad and ashamed about it, but I was too fuzzy-headed to know how to change anything.

Then came the turning point. My mum took me out on a shopping trip one day. As we left the shopping mall, the heavens opened and I was soaked to the skin. Within hours, I was shivering and sweating with fever. My mum insisted that I stay with her but, despite lots of tender loving care from her, after two days I was obviously seriously ill. Mum called an ambulance, and I was admitted into hospital with pneumonia. As always, Stan was there, acting the devoted husband and promising the hospital staff that he would take great care of me, should they allow me to go home.

I was in hospital for ten days, and during that time I wasn't given my usual dosage of antidepressants. I remember lying in the bed, looking at the other patients and watching their partners come and visit them with love and kind words of encouragement to get better. Yet when Stan came to visit he had nothing kind or warm to say and I would pretend to sleep, hoping that he would just go away.

This small act of defiance felt like a breakthrough for me since it was a decision I had made for myself. A few days later I went a step further. Mum and Dad brought the kids up to see me and I confided in Mum and told her I wanted to get away from Stan. She was shocked, but said she would support me in whatever decision I made. And with her on my side things started to change. When I was discharged I went home to my parents' house. The children were already there, so it was easier than I thought to make the change.

Stan was horrified when I said I was leaving him. He hounded me, trying, with threats, promises and pleadings, to talk his way back into my life. The months that followed weren't easy. To my family Stan had never been anything other than the perfect son-in-law, husband and father and it took a lot of time and talking before they understood how I felt. Of course it was my own fault, for covering up so well.

Once they did understand they backed me fully. And with their support, as well as having my kids with me and freedom from the hurt and humiliation that Stan inflicted, I began to recover.

I threw away the antidepressants and promised myself that I'd never take them again. I went out and got a new job, working in another estate agent's. And I went to a solicitor and said I wanted a divorce.

The more I regained control of my life, the more I felt the old me coming back. I was able to look after my kids properly for the first time, playing with them and taking them out to the park – simple things I had almost never done with them.

Of course, it wasn't all simple: there were scary times when I felt weak and the past would creep back into my head. Sometimes it was as if there were two people talking to me, the negative Judy and the positive Judy, but in the end the real, positive me triumphed.

Stan continued to hound me, trying to make me change my mind, but I knew I wouldn't. I didn't stop him seeing the children, in fact he still plays an active part in their lives. But I made sure that I was never alone with him. In many ways Stan wasn't a terrible man. He was a good father. But he had no idea how to relate to a woman: he didn't talk *to* me, he talked *at* me, always trying to control me. And sexually he was in the Dark Ages, somehow believing that my consent wasn't needed for him to do whatever he wanted.

I didn't think about prosecuting him – it was enough that I had got away. But with the law as it is now, if I were in that situation I would warn him that he could be jailed for what he was doing to me.

I think we brought out the worst in each other. He became a bully and I became a victim, living like a trapped animal without any sense of who I was.

Judy stopped and I thought about what she'd said. Sometimes we do bring out the worst in each other, but that seems a very generous assessment of a really horrible situation that almost cost Judy her mental health and her relationship with her children.

I asked her how things were with them now. 'Wonderful,' she replied, smiling. 'I've done my best to make up for the lost years, spending time with them, being involved in their lives and being there for them. They're great kids.'

And Stan?

'Once the divorce came through he finally accepted that it was over. Now I keep conversations with him brief – we only talk about the kids and arrangements we need to make. I'd rather avoid him totally, but I can't do that because of the kids. But we've both moved on and I've even met someone else. It's only recent, and after such a terrible marriage I'm going very, very slowly with this new man. I married Stan much too fast and I know now that you have to get past the initial starry-eyed bit and really get to know someone before you make any kind of commitment.'

Judy laughed, and I nodded agreement. She was right. Taking it slowly really is the key to avoiding mistakes. And if anyone deserves to get it right next time round it's Judy.

11
Debbie

Where hard drugs are concerned there is almost always abuse. Not only the abuse of the drugs themselves, but the abuse of vulnerable and innocent people by predators – the drug pushers and dealers. These people are responsible for endless amounts of misery and hopelessness, and often for death too.

Debbie was a girl who fell prey to the drug sharks, and almost paid for it with her life. She was a beautiful young woman with the world at her feet, yet drug addiction – and the people who fed her drugs – almost destroyed her.

Thankfully Debbie lived to fight back and to tell the tale. When I met her I was touched by her story, and I want to include it here because Debbie's story could happen to any bright, beautiful young girl who lands up in the wrong place at the wrong time.

I first met Debbie quite a few years back, when Alan and I went to visit his parents for the day. They lived in London's East End, where there was still a strong sense of community. Everyone knew everyone else and not much was private, but there was a lot of humour and support there too.

This particular day was hot and very sunny and I perched on the garden wall, eating an ice lolly and people-watching. Alan came to sit with me and as people passed by several of them recognised him and came to say hello.

One of them was a girl whom Alan introduced as 'little Debbie'. She had been at school with him, although she was a few years younger. I was completely taken by how beautiful she was.

Debbie was the younger sister of one of Alan's friends. He told me that she had always been very popular, and I could see why. As she walked off I remarked to Alan what a beauty she was – tall and very slim, with an amazing figure. Her long blonde hair hung down to her waist, shiny and healthy, and she had a heart-shaped face with green eyes and perfect teeth in a lovely smile.

Alan told me that she was the only girl in a family of five boys. Apparently she was the apple of her dad's eye, and he and her brothers were a little overprotective of her. She was bright and was at college studying art, while modelling part-time. She looked like a girl with the world at her feet.

Two years passed and on another visit to Alan's family, sitting once more on the front wall, we saw little Debbie again. But this time nothing could have prepared me for what I saw. At first I thought the girl we were looking at couldn't be the gorgeous creature we had chatted to before. But Alan insisted that she was, and that she had broken her father's heart and was now a very different girl. I could see that – but what had happened to her?

Alan waved to her and she waved back. But this time, rather than stopping to say hello, she scurried down the street, head down and shoulders hunched. Alan shook his head and went in to join the family while I stayed sitting on the wall, wondering about little Debbie.

An hour must have passed and just as I was about to go inside I saw Debbie's hunched figure heading back my way. Curiosity got the better of me and I called out and waved her over. She hesitated at first, but then came over and perched herself next to me on the wall.

I asked her if she remembered me and she nodded.

'Yes, I remember you. Everyone knows you're Martine's mum. She's brilliant and beautiful.'

I wanted to return the compliment, but I would have been lying. The transformation in Debbie was terrible. Her eyes were dull, her skin was sallow and pale and her teeth were blackened and chipped. Her beautiful long hair was limp and lifeless, and as she crossed her legs they looked like twigs, they were so thin. Only one thing could have brought about such a dramatic change – and I had little doubt that Debbie was on hard drugs.

I asked her if she was OK.

'Do I look it?' she snapped back. Then she softened. 'I'm sorry, I didn't mean to be rude, I'm just feeling a little under the weather and I'm hurting a bit. I know you disapprove, everyone does, but they don't understand. No one does. I'm on my own here, you know, and I can't stop,' she said. She gazed down at the pavement and then, to my surprise, kept talking. 'Everyone told me that education was good for me. I was so excited when I started college. I wanted to draw and paint and get into a trendy set. Big mistake.'

I said nothing, willing her to go on.

'Don't get me wrong, the first few weeks were amazing and I made lots of friends. One of them was Ian. He was always around and paid me a lot of attention. He wasn't really my type, but he was handsome and popular, and I suppose I was flattered that he liked me. We started going out and I remember we spent the evenings with friends, smoking dope, drinking wine or beer and thinking we were being really creative.

'Then one day Ian suggested I try something "a bit stronger". I wasn't sure, but he told me how wonderful the high was, how much I'd love it and how brilliant it would be for me as an artist, making me more creative and imaginative. He told me that all the stuff about getting hooked was exaggerated and I'd be fine.

'I believed him – and let him give me coke and later heroin. In a matter of weeks I was hooked and craving it every day. Ian was hooked, too – I just hadn't realised and I'd let him drag me in with him. I'd thought he was so cool, but he was just a sad drug addict who got me addicted too.

'Within a few months the drugs took over – I couldn't do without them and I couldn't manage college any more. I dropped out and moved in with Ian. Although I knew he'd got me hooked I wasn't willing to face that. He was my link to drugs, he knew the pushers and where we could get more at any time of the day or night, so I needed him.'

Debbie started rubbing her bony knees as if to try and warm herself up. It was a lovely day, but she was obviously cold and unwell.

'As time passed my so-called friends moved on,' she said. 'All except Ian. We stuck together because neither of us had anyone else. He's at home waiting for me now. He'll be in a state soon, so I can't be long. I'm often round here – my supplier lives up the road.'

Debbie looked at me for signs of disapproval, but I just nodded, giving nothing away.

'I hate him,' she burst out. 'But I don't blame him. He's just running a business, I suppose, and he does do me favours, but then I do favours for him too, if you get my drift.'

I looked up at her then. She was gazing into space. 'Do you mean sexual favours?' I asked her.

'Of course – what else? It's been hard to find the money sometimes and I'll do anything. My dealer never asks for full sex, it's normally just a blow job.

'It wasn't always that way. At first it was easy to

borrow money and my parents didn't suspect anything. They never really liked Ian, but when I asked them for something I usually got what I wanted. But I couldn't keep on borrowing without them suspecting, and in the end they found out.

'They tried to help me, and they've put up with a lot. I've lied and stolen from them, my brothers have paid visits to Ian and my dealer to try and frighten them into leaving me alone, but nothing works. Ian and I are stuck together, both of us hooked on the drugs, both of us needing the dealer.

'When all the other options ran out I started selling myself. It was easy, because back then I had something to sell. There's not many people want me now, apart from my dealer and even then I think he just feels sorry for me. I still get the odd client down Brick Lane, they seem less fussy, but I don't look too good any more and besides, not many men want to screw an addict. They seem to think that I might give them something.'

I asked Debbie about Ian. How did he feel about what she was doing? She laughed ruefully.

'If I were clean I doubt whether we'd be together. We fell into the trap at the same time. Now all we have left is each other and he's the only one who understands what I feel and vice versa. It's a vicious circle. We have our moments of normality when we both want something more, but they never last long enough for either of us to do anything about it. The craving takes over and all that matters is the next score.

'I sell myself to get the drugs for both of us. Ian knows that's what I do, which makes him a pimp.

'I know I can't go on like this for ever. I don't even want to. Perhaps I'll die, perhaps that's all there is, I don't know.'

Debbie stood up. 'I don't suppose you could give me some money for a packet of fags?'

She looked so hopeful that I couldn't say no. She took the ten-pound note I held out and said goodbye. I watched her skeletal frame as she walked down the road.

'Debbie,' I called after her. 'Make sure you spend it on cigarettes.' She turned and smiled.

'I will,' she said as she disappeared around the corner.

Some months passed and Alan and I were on our way back from a trip to London's West End one evening when we decided to take a detour from our usual route and stop off in Brick Lane to buy smoked salmon and salt-beef bagels. We'd been out to dinner at a very posh restaurant, but Al was starving and complaining that the restaurant portions had been too small. He really wanted to eat, and at that time of night the only place open was the bagel shop.

As we drove down Bethnal Green Road we passed the old railway arches, shrouded in shadows. On market days these are open and stallholders sell old furniture and clothes from them. But at night they're a haunt for prostitutes. As we approached, I realised that one of the girls standing by the arches was a familiar figure. 'Gosh, Al, it's young Debbie,' I exclaimed.

Alan shook his head despairingly. He had hoped that she might have come off drugs – and the streets – but it seemed she had not.

Debbie stayed on my mind for a long time afterwards. I couldn't forget the skinny shape lurking in the shadows, looking for customers.

Months later, close to Christmas, we paid another visit to Alan's family. It was miserable weather, damp and wet. I had forgotten to bring my cigarettes and decided to go to the local shop to buy some. The shop was fairly busy and as I waited to pay I heard a familiar voice. It was little Debbie.

'Jen,' she called.

I turned around, expecting the worst – and was both shocked and pleased by what I saw. It was obvious that Debbie had turned a significant corner. She looked so much better than when I had last seen her. I was intrigued to find out more, so when we left the shop we huddled together under the shop canopy, out of the rain, and talked. Despite the dismal day Debbie seemed happy and almost jubilant.

'Can't tell you how pleased I am to see you again.' Debbie turned from side to side, showing me the new person she now was. 'It's early days, but I feel great, and everything is going so well.' She hugged me and whispered in my ear. 'I've been clean for over four months and I'm back with Mum and Dad.'

Although I didn't know Debbie well I was overjoyed to see her back on track with her life. 'Let's nip into the café and have a cuppa,' I suggested. Debbie happily agreed and we settled into a quiet corner, cupping our hands around hot coffee mugs to warm them. 'So what happened?' I asked. 'Tell me the story.'

'It's weird, really, but after you showed me kindness something changed – I decided that I could get help.'

'Kindness?' I asked.

'I don't suppose you remember. But you loaned me money for cigarettes.'

Of course I remembered, but why had the small favour I'd done her made such an impact?

'I was touched that you gave it to me,' she said. 'Most people wouldn't have, knowing I'd probably spend it on drugs. Maybe it was because a stranger showed me kindness, I don't know, but by the time I got back to my flat I was quietly determined that the money you gave me wouldn't be put into the drug pusher's pocket.

'For days I held on to that ten-pound note, almost as if it was a lifeline. Every time I felt weak I would dig deep into my jacket pocket, feel the note and think of you and the conversation we had on the wall that day, and how you made me feel that there was a way out of the hell I was in. Don't get me wrong, there were many times after our meeting when I took drugs again. I carried on selling myself to get the money to pay for the drugs for me and Ian, but I never used that ten-pound note, ever!'

I mentioned that I had seen her down at the arches one night. Debbie's face saddened at the reminder of the many nights she had spent there and I knew that she would have to deal with the memory of a lot of bad things that had happened to her.

I told her a little about my own past. She seemed shocked and surprised when I told her how I had been abused as a young woman and how I had been raped and beaten. It seemed to put her at ease, realising that I had been in a dark and difficult place too.

'It's funny you should tell those things,' she said. 'Somehow I knew from our first meeting that you had suffered too. You never judged me and I could see you wanted to help me.

'What really made me wake up to everything, though, was what happened to Ian. It was one night a few months back, when I got home after work. I'd been to the usual haunts and one punter, the last of the evening, had been particularly hard to please. I don't want to go into detail, but he was rough and harsh, he had bitten me, and I was bruised and hurting by the time I got back to our flat.

'Ian was curled up on the sofa in a foetal position. He was unusually quiet, but to be honest I didn't take a lot of notice. I needed a bath and although I called to him a few times it wasn't until I sat down with a drink that I realised something was wrong. He was barely breathing and was deathly pale. I called an ambulance and went with him to hospital. It was too late. Ian died that night. He had taken too much gear, drunk heavily and then choked on his own vomit. The next few days were really terrible and all a bit surreal in fact. I could never have coped without my family. During those dark days Mum and Dad took over. They took me home, fed me, comforted me and reassured me that I could get through it and I would be all right.

'I cried a lot, first for Ian, and then thinking of all the terrible things I had put my parents through. Yet they forgave me and only wanted to help.

'I don't remember Ian's funeral or the inquest or anything. I think I just floated through it all, barely there. My family didn't go – they blamed Ian for getting me onto drugs and although they'd never wanted him dead they were grateful that he was no longer around me. I understood how they felt about him, but for me it was harder. I kept remembering the times when I'd first met him – he was so different then – and wondering what happened and how we ended up the way we did.

'Mum and Dad got me into rehab and stuck by me while I went through the painful weeks of drug withdrawal. It was tough, the toughest thing I've ever done, but I was determined to make it out the other side. I knew I didn't want to end up like Ian, I wanted a life, and rehab was the price I had to pay.

'I came out six months ago and I'm still clean. I take it a day at a time and I got to meetings of NA – Narcotics Anonymous – almost every day. I meet people there who've been through the same thing and it gives me the support I need to say no to drugs.

'I've even signed on for a new college course. Not art this time, but business studies. I can't wait to start.'

Debbie smiled and when I looked at her heart-shaped face I saw hope. She didn't have all the answers and it was early days for her, but the hope was there and I so wanted her to continue with the good life she now had. Debbie told me she had to go – she was worried that she would be late getting back to her parents.

'I don't go out that often on my own. Mum and Dad still worry and I don't want them getting concerned. Thanks for listening, Jen.' She promised to stay in touch and I wished her well before she slipped out of the café into the rain. As I got up to leave, I noticed that Debbie had left a packet of cigarettes on the table. Had this been a little thank-you from her? I put them in my bag, paid the bill and made my way back to Alan's family's house.

Just before Alan and I moved to France we paid another visit to his family to say our farewells and once again I saw Debbie. Over a year had passed since our chat in the café and she looked like a million dollars. Her long blonde hair was shorter but was shining and healthy once more. Cosmetic dental surgery had restored her beautiful smile and her skin was glowing. She looked like the old Debbie I had first seen all those years ago.

We only chatted briefly as we were outside and it was January and very cold. She told me all about her recovery and how well she felt. She was doing well at college and had a new boyfriend. As we said our goodbyes, she held on to my hand for a moment longer, telling me that she had something to show me. Out from the side zipper of her purse she produced a ten-pound note. 'I never used it, and if you don't mind, I'd like to keep it. It's like my lucky charm. Something changed the day you gave me this, and I really don't want to part with it.'

I smiled at her and said, 'You keep it, Debbie – you deserve all the luck in the world'.

12
Colin

Colin's story is about the abuse of a child by an adult in a position of trust and authority. There are few worse crimes. Parents can't be with their children twenty-four hours a day: they have to trust the qualified people in whose care they leave their children – whether these are teachers, priests, Scoutmasters or carers. Such people are qualified to look after children and, parents believe, should treat their small charges with kindness and respect. In the vast majority of cases parents' trust is well-placed and appropriate. Most of those who care for our children are good people who would never harm them. But there are, sadly, exceptions. Among the trustworthy there is, from time to time, someone whose behaviour is so appalling that it is almost beyond belief.

The repercussions when a child is abused by such an authority figure are enormous, for the child, for the parents and wider family, and for those who employed and worked with the wrongdoer. As Colin's story shows, the ripples of the after-effects can spread very wide and can go on spreading for years.

Colin was married to a girl I used to go to dance

lessons with, many years ago. Sheila and I stayed in touch and once I married Alan the four of us became good friends.

Colin is a big man: over six feet tall and stocky, with broad shoulders, he certainly isn't a fellow whom many people would like to cross. I can still remember him arm-wrestling with Alan, who is also incredibly strong. Alan struggled to beat him and only managed it when Colin, who is right-handed, used his left arm.

Before we moved to France Alan and I would often go out with Colin and Sheila. They were always great fun and we had many a good evening out at our local restaurants and pubs in Essex.

Colin has always been chatty, with a quick sense of humour and a joke in virtually every sentence. He is very much the outdoor type, someone who enjoys camping and fishing – what I would call a real man's man, but with a kind, sensitive and romantic side to his nature. Sheila has received flowers every Saturday since they met, and he never forgets a birthday or anniversary.

One evening when Alan and I were back in England on holiday after the publication of *Behind Closed Doors*, we were invited round to Colin and Sheila's house for dinner. We hadn't seen one another for a while so there was lots to catch up on. We had a lovely relaxing evening, with great home cooking, good wine and lots of laughter. We talked about all kinds of things, as always, from our kids and jobs to the state of the world.

As the evening wore on we got onto the subject of religion. In the middle of a heated debate about religion and war Colin mentioned that he was a Catholic. 'Really?' I said. 'I didn't know that, but then I suppose the subject has never come up before. Is your religion important to you?'

'Not now,' Colin replied. 'But it was once. My mum was very religious and insisted that we all went to Mass every Sunday and joined the choir – I sang in my local church choir for four years.'

We all laughed at the image of big, manly Colin as a choirboy. Colin joined in the laughter, but then he became very quiet. Sheila went to fetch another bottle of wine and Alan asked him if he was all right.

'Yes, mate, I'm OK,' Colin said. 'It's just that there are some painful memories for me around those days.' He paused and Alan and I waited, not sure whether to change the subject or not.

'Oh, what the heck, I might as well tell you about it,' Colin said. 'It was all a long time ago, but it had a huge effect on me. I don't talk about it to many people, but I know you two so well, and I thought your book was great, Jenny, so I don't mind telling you.'

Sheila came back in and poured us all another glass of wine as Colin began.

'Do you remember a story in the papers some years ago, about a Father Dominic who was found guilty of abusing seven boys and was suspected of abusing many more? It was about ten years ago and the trial was in the paper for days.'

We had to admit that although it rang a bell with us we couldn't remember much about it.

'Well, I was part of that story,' Colin said. 'You see, that man was the priest at my local church and I was one of the boys he abused.'

Both Alan and I were stunned. It was hard to believe that a priest, who is supposed to represent all that is good, could commit such a crime. But we knew from the deadly serious look on Colin's face that he was telling the truth.

'What happened?' Alan asked. 'How did he get away with it?'

'Only too easily,' Colin said grimly. 'You see, my parents trusted him totally – all the parents did. They left us in his care without a moment's worry. A priest was considered beyond the desires of the flesh, beyond sin – after all, he was the one who absolved the sins of others, at confession. Colin sighed and continued his story.

I was one of six kids and we were all involved in the Church from the beginning. Dad wasn't as devout as Mum – she went to Mass three times a week – but he was happy for her to cart us all off to church on a Sunday and he trusted the priests as much as she did.

Father Dominic was a youngish priest who had been at that particular church for a few years. Of course, since I was only a child myself I didn't think he was young but when all the details came out later I realised he had only been thirty-two when I joined the choir as a seven-year-old.

Mum was over the moon when I got into the choir. My older brother Michael had failed to get in, so I was fulfilling her dream. And because she was so pleased and excited, I was too. I got to wear my little white ruffled collar and surplice and I looked angelic, though outside the church I was just the same scruffy, snot-nosed, loud-mouthed kid as all the rest.

I had to go to choir practice every week and then sing at services as well as special occasions like weddings and funerals. It took up a lot of time, but luckily one of my best friends, Sid, was in the choir too. We used to whisper jokes and share sweets to pass the time.

Father Dominic didn't take choir practice, we had a choirmaster for that – Mr Regan. He was very exacting, but a good musician and we liked him. Father Dominic would often be lurking around during practice and we were always a bit intimidated by him – we'd had it drummed into us that he was the next thing to God, so you can imagine how in awe of him we were.

Father Dominic knew us all and it wasn't unusual for him to ask one or other of us to run errands or do small chores for him. He knew that our parents would be only too pleased to have us help. I lived in the next street to the church, so I was allowed to walk there on my own and to go home alone at the end. So it was easy – and beyond suspicion – for Father Dominic to call me aside just before I left and ask me to pop into his private office with him.

Believe it or not, I was a cute little boy. I had blond curls and a butter-wouldn't-melt expression. And Father Dominic liked me, or so I thought. He would often pat me on the head or make some flattering comment about my singing or what a good boy I was and my mother would almost swoon with delight when I told her.

I'd been in the choir for about six months when Father Dominic began asking me to stay behind almost every week. He gave me little jobs to do – going to the corner shop for some milk for him, or putting away a pile of prayer books. After I'd done the job he'd give me a biscuit and tell me how good I was. I was always desperate to go home, I didn't like having to stay, but I was far too much in awe of him to say anything. I did as I was told and when Father Dominic told me to come and sit beside him, even though I didn't want to, I obediently did as I was told.

When he began to fondle me, first stroking my leg and then going a lot further, I was so shocked that I simply let him. The first time I thought I must have dreamed it, but he began doing it every week, eventually masturbating me and then getting me to masturbate him. I didn't know what to think, but he swore me to silence, telling me that God knew I was a good boy and that what happened was private, only between us, because I was so special.

I didn't want to be special. I remember wondering if God really thought it was OK, and thinking that He surely couldn't. I didn't dare say a word to anyone – I was far too scared of Father Dominic – and in any case I was sure they'd never believe me. But at night in bed I prayed for it to stop, begging God to make Father Dominic leave me alone, bargaining with God that if He'd only make it stop I'd do a thousand good deeds.

As weeks and then months went by and Father Dominic went on abusing me, I despaired. Why couldn't God hear me? I wondered. Or did He *want* these horrible things to happen?

I begged my mum to let me leave the choir, but of course she wouldn't hear of it. I skipped choir practice a couple of times, but Father Dominic would always tell her and then I'd get a hiding.

The abuse went on for four years, until I was eleven. As I grew older it happened less often: I think Father Dominic became nervous that I might tell and besides, as I realised later, he had other young victims in his sights. But he wasn't about to let me go easily. He wanted to keep control, and he went on grabbing me after choir practice, taking me into his office to indulge his sick appetites and then swearing me to silence, a sickly smile on his face.

In the end I knew that I couldn't take it any more. I

told my mother I was leaving the choir and nothing she did would make me go back. I'd rather have taken any number of hidings than more abuse. Mum could see that I meant it and she gave in, though she huffed and puffed about it for ages.

Once I realised that I wouldn't have to go back I was so happy. I felt a huge cloud of fear and dread lift. But I wasn't completely free – I still had to see Father Dominic at church on Sunday and sometimes in the street. He'd ruffle my hair and ask me why I'd left the choir, fixing his stare on me so intensely that all I could do was look at the floor and mumble that I had a lot of things going on at school. I hated meeting him – my stomach lurched every time I saw him, his black gown flapping about his legs.

Two years later he was moved to another church. No one knew why – it was very sudden. I remember my mother saying that he was such a good man that they must need him elsewhere. She even went up to the church with a leaving gift for him.

At the time I was so relieved that I didn't care why he'd gone. It was only years later that I learned a complaint had been made against him by the parents of another boy he was abusing, and he'd been moved hastily to avoid a scandal.

I tried to forget about Father Dominic, but what he had done to me had changed me. I felt ashamed, disgusted and disillusioned. I hated him because he'd taken away my innocence and shown me the seamy side of life – and because he'd had such power over me.

For years I put what he'd done to the back of my mind. I was always outgoing and that hadn't changed: I went round with a crowd of friends, dated girls and eventually met Sheila. But I couldn't get rid of the memories and the feeling that Father Dominic shouldn't have got away with it.

It was Sheila who said to me one day, 'You don't have to let him get away with it.' Do you know, until then it hadn't occurred to me that there was anything I could do. But when she said that it was as if a light went on. I thought about it for days. I had no idea where he was, but I could tell the police what had happened and at least try to get *some* justice.

For years I believed that I was the only one he'd abused. But talking to Sheila I realised that I probably wasn't the only one. Why would I be, when he had access to lots of small boys all the time? When I realised that he might still be doing it I knew that I had to act.

The day I walked into my local police station I didn't know if I was crazy or not. Would they listen, or just laugh at me? I just knew I had to try. I was thirty-three and it was twenty years since I'd last seen Father Dominic. But if he was still out there I was going to do my best to nail him.

The police were great. They did listen, and they promised to investigate. They kept me informed and a few weeks later my police liaison officer told me that they'd found another man who said he'd been abused by Father Dominic as a boy – the one whose parents' complaint had led to Father Dominic being moved when I was thirteen. I was jubilant: it was as though I could be sure, for the first time in all those years, that I really wasn't mad or making it up.

The police investigation went on for two years and by the end of that time they had found seven men willing to testify against Father Dominic and several more who had been abused by him but didn't want to testify. Father Dominic was still a priest and when they arrested him it hit the headlines.

The court case went on for weeks and I was one of those who testified. I was so nervous that I could barely stand up in the witness box but I was determined to go through with it and I did. I stood in that courtroom and looked at him and instead of the big scary priest I remembered I saw a pathetic, scrawny man of fifty-something who couldn't look me in the eye. I wasn't scared at all: I stood in the witness box and told the court exactly what he'd done to me for four years.

At the end of the trial Father Dominic got seven years in prison. I think he should have got a lot longer, but at least that was something. And of course he lost everything – his position, his job and the respect of all those people who'd known him and looked up to him over the years.

The day he went down I planned to celebrate. But in

the end I didn't feel like breaking open the champagne – it was a fitting end to a sad story and I was just glad it was all over.

Sheila was wonderful. She backed me and stood by me through it all, listening, holding my hand and looking after me. I couldn't have done it without her.

There was one thing I had to do that was almost harder than anything else, and that was to tell my mum. She had to know, and I wanted to tell her before it hit the papers. I knew that it would shatter her faith in the Church, and I was afraid, deep down, that she might not believe me.

I went round to see her one day and told her the whole story. When I'd finished she put her head in her hands and cried. Then she hugged me and said how sorry she was and that she wished she had known. By the time she'd finished both of us had tears streaming down our faces and we could hardly speak. It meant the world to me that she had never doubted me.

My mother was actually amazingly strong, all through the trial. And, surprisingly, it didn't shatter her faith: she's still very involved with the Church. The way she saw it, Father Dominic was a bad apple but that didn't mean the whole barrel was bad – and she was right: there are plenty of genuinely good priests out there.

As Colin ended his story Alan and I told him how brave we thought he was to have gone to the police. He had helped not only himself but Father Dominic's other victims – past, present and future.

'Yes, it made me happy to think that he'd never hurt a child again,' Colin agreed. 'It's ten years since he went to jail, so he's probably out by now, but no one will ever let him go near a kid again.

'For me, the trial and the prison sentence put the whole thing to rest. I've slept a lot easier since then. I carried that secret around for twenty years, but once it was out, and not a secret any more, I was free to get on with my life.'

13
Grace

Grace was a smashing lady and a good friend. I met her through Martine, as the two of them were very good friends. Grace had parted from her husband and brought her children up alone. She was always busy and reminded me of myself in the days when Martine was small and I was a single parent. I used to hold down three different jobs to make ends meet, and I spent life rushing from one to the next while doing my best to be there for Martine as much of the time as I could. Grace was the same, always on the go but devoted to her kids.

Grace and I often went out for lunch together when I was living in London. We would sit in Wimbledon Village and chat about almost everything – but most of all about our kids. Grace had four children so there was lots to talk about. Three of them were grown up and had moved away from home, but her youngest daughter, Ellie, was still living with Grace.

Ellie was a beautiful girl with long blonde hair, massive blue eyes and perfect teeth. At fourteen she looked much older than she was and was the apple of Grace's eye. As far as Grace was concerned, nothing was too much trouble for Ellie. Grace worked long hard hours and a lot of what she earned went on Ellie.

Grace had a lovely soft way about her. She was warm and caring and a very good listener, always ready with a shoulder for her friends to lean on if things got tough. But, despite being quite a soft-hearted person, Grace didn't shy away from fighting a battle, especially if it was on behalf of any of her children. Like many mothers, she could turn into a tigress if she thought that anyone was going to hurt or take advantage of one of her babies.

There was a big gap between Ellie and the next-oldest sister, so Ellie was still only nine by the time the others had all left home. She and Grace had always been close, but they became even closer and had a lot of fun. Grace told me how they used to giggle together all the time and go on outings – a picnic in the park, swimming or ice skating.

That was why it was such a shock for Grace when things began to change and Ellie became more and more distant. As the problems developed and grew worse, Grace found it hard to take in that her sweet child was gradually becoming an impossible, aggressive monster.

Any parent will be able to imagine Grace's grief and distress at the events that unfolded over the next few years as she gradually felt Ellie slipping away from her and became the victim of her daughter's violence. And that's why I want to tell Grace's story, because there but for a twist of fortune goes any one of us. No one imagines that their beloved child will turn against them, or that the toddler who couldn't bear to be out of their sight might one day become a snarling, angry, violent teenager. But sometimes it happens – and for those parents who are on the receiving end it becomes a nightmare of self-blame, anxiety, hopes raised and dashed over and over again, and a desperate wish to turn the clock back.

Since the beginning of Grace's problems I have been there for her, either in person or over the phone, and I have witnessed at first hand the changes in Ellie and the trouble and heartache that Grace has endured. Not only has she seen her precious daughter change beyond recognition, but she has been let down time and time again by the authorities to whom she went for help and support. At every turn she was met by a wall of so-called professionals who did nothing but add to the trauma as she tried to do what was right for her child.

The story began a few years ago, when Ellie started secondary school. Grace says that she spotted the difference in her attitude in the first week. Ellie's closest friend, a lovely girl, had moved away over the summer and Ellie made friends with two girls who had been troublemakers when they were all at junior school together. Almost from the start of her first term at the new school Ellie began to disobey her mother, answer back and refuse to do her homework.

As the months passed, Ellie changed more and more.

The sweet, sunny child she had been was replaced by a surly, grumpy, rude girl who began to skip school, hitch up the skirt of her uniform far too high and hang out in the evenings with the girls whom Grace had always tried to avoid.

It wasn't long before a letter arrived from the school, telling Grace that Ellie had missed several classes. Grace had suspected as much and was mortified. Ellie's attendance at junior school had been exemplary – Grace had always made sure that her daughter was at school on time and well turned-out – and she found it hard to cope with the fact that Ellie was now rejecting what her mother had always taught her.

Grace decided to speak with her daughter to try and find out what the problem was. They had always been able to talk and had shared many special conversations in the past, so Grace was absolutely amazed when Ellie refused to sit down with her and discuss anything. In fact, Ellie had shouted at her mother, telling her to shut her face and keep out of her life. Shaken and worried, Grace went to see Ellie's teachers, who told her that Ellie was just as rude at school and that they were concerned about her. After that things really started to deteriorate. Over the following months Grace got used to the letters and phone calls from the school, reporting that Ellie was not attending regularly, not doing homework and was misbehaving during school hours.

Grace's heart sank when she was told that her daughter had been caught smoking behind the school buildings, and had been involved in a fight. Ellie was suspended for a week, but it made no difference – she was just pleased to be off school and didn't care about her mother's feelings or her own damaged prospects.

After the suspension Ellie didn't even bother to try to deceive her mother into believing that she was going to school. When Grace arrived home from her early-morning cleaning job Ellie was often still in bed and nothing Grace said or did seemed to affect her.

Grace had tried everything she could think of, from stopping Ellie's pocket money to grounding her and taking away her most precious possessions. But none of it worked. Ellie just seemed to get more and more defiant and angry and Grace spent many evenings on the phone to friends, asking for advice.

Everything possible was done to try and coax Ellie back into her education programme. The school had talked to her, punished her, offered incentives and moved her class. Grace, increasingly worried, gave up her morning cleaning job so that she could take Ellie to school herself. She got Ellie into the car, took her to the school and even walked with her to the classroom in an effort to ensure her attendance. It wasn't easy, because Ellie swore at her and shouted as Grace ordered her into the car, but Grace had realised she had to develop a thick hide when it came to Ellie's fury.

Grace could see Ellie into school but she couldn't make her stay there, and most days Ellie, who had no respect for her teachers or fellow pupils, would leave the school building and disappear soon after Grace left. By the time Grace got home, the phone would be ringing to say that Ellie had walked out and was once more absent from school. Short of standing outside the school all day, Grace was beaten. The final blow came when, after countless meetings with the teachers and headmaster and a further suspension, the school decided to expel Ellie.

After this events descended from worrying to tragic in a short space of time. Grace's description of what followed, and what she went through, is both moving and poignant.

I couldn't believe the transformation in Ellie. It seemed that one minute she was this wonderful, beautiful girl who would do anything for me, and in the next breath she became an absolute monster. I have struggled to find out what caused this change in my lovely daughter and I keep looking to myself to see what I did wrong. I tried so hard with her, and yet I can't help feeling that I failed.

It's funny how as mothers we believe that when things go wrong for our children it's due to something that we've done. It's taken me a long time to come to terms with what Ellie put me through, but she is my daughter and I knew I would stick by her no matter what she did.

When Ellie was expelled I was beside myself. She

had been so excited about secondary school – I honestly believed that she was going to settle in and enjoy her school years, as her older brothers and sister had done. Ellie and I had always been so close and I had always thought that she would confide in me if she had troubles. But I was wrong.

I learned eventually that Ellie had befriended some kids in an older class. This didn't surprise me, since she was always much more mature than the average twelve-year-old, but I was totally unprepared for the three years that followed.

Although Ellie was enrolled in a new school her behaviour stayed the same and she was soon expelled again. She was put into a special study programme for school absconders, but most of the time she refused to turn up even for that.

I was worried sick about the education that she was missing and what would become of her. But the biggest shock was finding out when she was thirteen that she had a boyfriend – and had become sexually active.

Although I knew she was hanging around with this older crowd in the evenings I still believed – foolishly, perhaps – that Ellie was basically a good girl and wouldn't do anything too extreme. When I discovered, by overhearing her on the phone when she was talking to a friend, that she was having sex I was horrified. As far as I was concerned she was still a baby and I was mortified that she even *knew* about sex. I tried all I could to sit her down and explain that she had many years ahead of her in which to have boyfriends and sex. But Ellie was having none of it – she told me to shut up and get a life.

I suppose that it was around this time that she first got physical with me. It all started off with me trying to talk to her before she left the house to go and meet her boyfriend. I knew nothing about who he was – she wouldn't tell me – and I was determined that she wouldn't go. But a scuffle started which ended with Ellie slapping my face and knocking me to the floor. As she slammed the front door I picked myself up, wondering what on earth had just happened. I felt bruised and hurt, but mostly my heart ached. This couldn't possibly be the behaviour of my little girl.

I felt terribly alone with it all. Ellie's dad wasn't in the picture – he'd gone off with someone else and hardly ever contacted his kids – and I had no close family to support me. Friends were fantastic but they couldn't be there with me every day, holding my hand.

I felt so low about it all that I went on antidepressants for a while and lost a lot of weight. I would sit in the house in the evening, wondering where Ellie was and worrying myself sick that something awful would happen to her.

After talking with you, Jen, and with other friends, I finally realised that the situation was beyond my control. Ellie had no respect for me, I couldn't talk to her, she was getting no education and she had a boyfriend who was breaking the law by having sex with her. I knew I needed help and I didn't know where to turn. On the advice of a friend I decided to contact social services.

Nothing could have prepared me for the way I was dealt with. After telling a duty social worker all that had happened, I was told that there was little I could do and that they didn't want to become involved with us as they felt that it would do more harm than good. I left with a few leaflets about teenage sex and a few numbers for some charity organisations. I couldn't believe it.

Over the coming weeks my concern for Ellie increased. She had started staying away from home and would disappear for days on end. I was frantic with worry about her. I went out in the car of a night looking for her and eventually found some of her friends. I managed to find out where her boyfriend lived and when I went to his address a very bedraggled Ellie opened the door.

As I took in the sight of my daughter I could feel the shock and anger welling up inside me. She was dirty and had a vacant expression on her face. In that moment I knew that she had been taking drugs – the signs were all too obvious. I demanded that she get her stuff and come home with me, but she laughed and told me to fuck off, before slamming the door in my face. I sobbed as I banged on the door and begged her to come home. But my cries went unheard and eventually I left, feeling sick and exhausted.

I was frightened by what was happening to Ellie and was determined to get her back. My next port of call was the police. As I queued at the station I felt sure that they could do something to help me. After all, Ellie was young and gullible and was being controlled by an older boy who was having sex with her and feeding her drugs.

When I reached the desk a kindly woman officer told me that despite wanting to help me they could not. As I sat with my mouth open in disbelief she said that they had no power to act. Ellie was not a runaway nor was she in any sort of trouble with the law. She had done nothing criminal. Even when I said that Ellie was taking drugs and having under-age sex, the officer replied that they could not intervene as it would be an intrusion into my daughter's life and that, again, nothing illegal could be proved.

I was still in a daze when I bumped into a friend of mine. Jan could see how distressed I was and took me back to her house for a coffee. I poured out the whole story and sobbed uncontrollably. How could my thir-teen-year-old be in an older boy's house, taking drugs and having sex, without anyone being able to stop it? No one seemed to care. Jan listened patiently and made me more coffee until I realised it was early evening. Thanking Jan for her support I made my way home. I still hoped that Ellie would come back, if for nothing more than a change of clothes, and I wanted to be there when she did.

As I approached the house, I saw that the lights were on. Ellie must be there. I felt both pleased and anxious – would I be able to persuade her to stay? But as I approached the door and saw that the glass panel had been smashed, panic set in. It wasn't Ellie, I thought – I must have been burgled. I called the police, telling them that I was frightened to go into my own house because I didn't know whether the intruders were still there. For the first time since I had given up smoking I felt like having a cigarette!

I waited in the street until the police finally arrived. Two officers told me to wait while they entered the house. When they at last reappeared they said that there had been a break-in and that I should contact my insurers. They gave me a crime number: there was little more that they could do so they left. I was alone. Cautiously, I went inside.

The house had been trashed. The contents of the drawers and shelves in each room were strewn over the floors. When I entered my bedroom I knew immediately that my jewellery had been taken. Back in the kitchen I checked the teapot where I kept cash for bills and realised that the money had gone too. Not much else had been stolen.

With a heavy heart I phoned the police to list the missing items. Then I began the enormous job of clearing up. Suddenly, out of the corner of my eye, I noticed Ellie's puffa jacket. For a second it didn't sink in. Ellie had been wearing that jacket the last time she'd left the house – which meant that she must have come back. Had she come in before the thieves arrived? Or – my stomach turned as the realisation hit me – had this been Ellie's work? Was my daughter the thief who had robbed me and wrecked the house? And, if so, why had she caused such devastation when she knew where my jewellery and the money were and could have just taken them? Did she hate me so much that she wanted to wreck our home? And if she did, then why?

I checked Ellie's room and found that most of her clothes had gone. It confirmed my worst fears – I sat in the lounge in the middle of a pile of books, broken ornaments and smashed CDs and sobbed until I felt I had run out of tears. What made me cry most of all was that Ellie had taken her old teddy bear. Under the angry, lost teenager she really was just a little girl still. I knew that I had to do whatever it took to get her back and away from this boy who had stolen her innocence, her joy in life and her future.

I rang the police and told them that I knew who had robbed me and I didn't want to press charges. I wasn't yet ready to prosecute my own daughter. I decided that night that I would let out my house and rent a new house in a nicer area where I knew there was a very good school. It was not too far away so I would still be able to see my friends, but was a good distance from the area that Ellie was hanging out in.

In the weeks that followed I made my preparations.

If Ellie was going to get her life back then I needed to play her at her own game. I began pretending that I was not bothered by her actions and had accepted the situation, and when she saw this she started to return home more often. There were times when I thought that my heart would break. She often came home dirty and I was sure her boyfriend had been beating her. She only came when she wanted something, but it was a start, and I was grateful for any small connection I could keep with her.

I continued to hound social services and the education authority for help, but still they wouldn't act and eventually I accepted that I had to sort things out alone. On one of Ellie's visits home I told her that I was moving and that she had to come with me. I was determined to hold my ground and to make sure that she did what she was told.

I was totally unprepared for what happened next. Ellie turned on me and started punching my face and body while screaming terrible abuse at me. She told me that I was responsible for everything that was wrong in her life. I was amazed at her strength, but finally I managed to get her off me. My mouth was bleeding and I could feel that one of my eyes was swollen. In my daze, I didn't see her reach for a knife and within seconds she had it at my throat.

You can't begin to imagine how I felt. I was terrified of my own child and of what she would do next. We stayed that way for what were probably seconds but which felt like hours. Then she finally let the knife fall from her hands and began to sob. I swept her into my arms, held her tight and told her how much I loved and missed her.

In that terrible moment of desperation, a light came on and I knew that the real Ellie was still there and that I was right never to have given up on her. We talked that night for the first time in over two years. Ellie did agree to move with me, but it wasn't the end of our troubles. It's been two years since we moved, Ellie is now fifteen and I'm only just beginning to feel that there is a light at the end of the tunnel.

In the past two years there have been many battles. Ellie did try to leave her boyfriend and come off drugs, but she left home and went back to him – and to the drugs – many times. She was violent towards me on several more occasions and left me bruised and battered. Each time I considered walking away from her, but as a mother I couldn't. Shocking as her behaviour was, I knew that it was only one side of Ellie, a side ruled by drugs and fear and anger.

On the positive side, Ellie did start at the new school and tried to adapt to it and to new friends, but she found it hard.

I try to take her out with me and her brother and sisters are always willing to keep an eye on her. But at the end of the day she needs to get her life back herself.

I took Ellie to see a counsellor and that has been a help. We found someone through a local organisation that was set up to help twelve to twenty-five-year-olds with problems and that's been good. While Ellie went to see the youth counsellor I went to see someone myself. I needed the support, and I wanted to know if I was to blame for what had happened and if I could have done anything better.

Ellie and I have talked about our counselling. She is very angry about my split with her dad. She blamed me, although it was him who had left us, and it had hit her hard when her brothers and sister had left. 'I've spent my whole life with people leaving me,' she said and I could see what she meant. As all this came out she began to see that I was the person who *hadn't* left her, who loved her enough to stay, no matter what. And through my counselling I began to accept that, although it might not have been perfect, I had always done my best for Ellie and I could do no more.

I have tried to keep optimistic and I'm so grateful to all my friends for the support they've shown. But I certainly can't say the same for the authorities who simply washed their hands of us.

Ellie's new school has been marvellous: her teachers keep me informed if she is missing lessons or doesn't turn up, and when she does go missing I often find her just wandering around. The low-life boyfriend has now gone, but Ellie still finds it hard to focus and to stay at school for the whole day. I worry sometimes that the drugs have done permanent damage, but doctors tell me that she is young and strong and will recover fully.

I live with a calmer, less volatile Ellie now and I'm grateful for that, though she's got a long way to go to get back on track with her studies and with being an ordinary fifteen-year-old. Sometimes I get a glimpse of the old Ellie, which gives me the strength to know that she is still there and worth fighting for.

The other evening she came, quite unexpectedly, and hugged me before she went up to bed, and said, 'I love you, Mum.' I felt the tears well up. There was a time when I wasn't sure that I would ever again feel her arms around me. Or hear those words.

Hearing Grace's story of her troubles with Ellie made me realise how very lucky I had been with my own daughter. Perhaps because she was so single-minded about her dreams and determined to succeed, Martine was never in any kind of trouble. She just wasn't interested in drugs or drink and even boys took a back seat to her work.

I liked to think, too, that the bond between us was so close that we could talk about anything. I would have been broken-hearted if she had kept troubles or problems from me and we had grown apart. Like Grace, I know that I would never have given up on a beloved child. But I'm very grateful that I didn't have to face that particular challenge in life.

Grace's story made me realise that every one of our

children is vulnerable. No matter how hard we try to give them stability and a solid base, once they reach their teens there are other influences in their lives. As parents we can only do our best – and keep on loving them, no matter what.

14
Linda

The tragedy of AIDS and HIV, the virus that causes it, is a tale of our times. This cruel disease, which carries with it a death sentence, can be passed on by a carrier without the recipient's knowledge. That means it's up to carriers to behave responsibly, inform partners and take precautions. But, sadly, some don't, either through ignorance or malice, and the consequences are enormous for all concerned.

There are cases of people who have been imprisoned for knowingly spreading the HIV virus. Their victims' lives have been wrecked when they have discovered they too are now HIV-positive and at risk of developing full-blown AIDS. And the added knowledge that this was done to them knowingly, by someone they were supposedly close to, only compounds the hurt and bewilderment of the news.

I'd heard about such cases but, like many tragedies, it was 'out there', happening to other people – until I met Linda.

Linda was a striking-looking woman in her late twenties. Long auburn hair fell in ringlets around her shoulders and she had the most amazing green eyes. I first met her through a friend and I liked her immediately. Warm and outgoing, she was an easy person to be with and over the next few months we saw quite a bit of one another. Linda had two lovely sons: Jamie, who was a six-year-old dynamo, and two-year-old Josh, who was a much quieter, more delicate-looking child. She was on her own with the boys, having parted from her husband a year earlier, so she had her hands full.

I had known Linda for some time before she told me that she was HIV-positive. She mentioned it one day, almost casually, when we were talking about health. I had been for a check-up because I suffer from diabetes, and after I had told her about it she mentioned that she had just been for a check-up herself. 'I've had it for about three years,' she said.

'That means Josh . . .' I paused, but Linda knew what I was asking.

'Yes,' she said quietly. 'He's got it too, Jen, and his health is a lot more frail than mine. I'm doing fine, but he already needs more intensive treatment. That's my biggest regret, that my little one has it. If only I'd known that I had it before I conceived him.'

'You didn't know?' I must have looked incredulous.

'No,' Linda said. 'I had no idea. I was in what I thought was a faithful marriage. Turned out that I was the one being faithful – but I couldn't have been more wrong about him.'

'Did he know that he had the virus?' I asked.

'Yes,' Linda replied. 'Unbelievably, he did. He had been going for counselling about it, before he passed it to me.'

'I'd really like to hear the whole story,' I told her. 'It seems so incredible that one person could do that to another, let alone a husband to a wife. What could have been going on in his head?'

'I've asked myself that many times,' Linda said. 'Yes, you can hear the story. I don't broadcast it, but I'm quite willing to tell it, especially when I think it might help others in some way.'

We were curled up on the sofa in my living room, sharing a bottle of wine. Linda's children were away on a weekend with their grandparents and she had some free time, and since my husband was abroad on business I did too so I'd invited her over for a meal.

I poured us both another glass of wine and Linda began her story.

I first met Rod when I was nineteen and he was twenty-two. That was ten years ago, when we both worked for the same company. We got together at the Christmas party – corny but true – and it just seemed so right. After that we were inseparable and a year later we were married.

With hindsight perhaps it was too soon. We were still in the first flush of love and there was so much that I didn't yet know about Rod – more than I could have imagined, in fact. But back then I thought I knew him so well and I thought that he was perfect for me.

Looking back, I realise that there was always a secretive side to Rod. He could be evasive, he liked a lot of 'space' – which meant time to himself – and he didn't talk a lot about his past or his childhood.

On the plus side, he could be funny and entertaining, we shared a lot of interests and he always did his share at home. In fact, other girls thought he was a model husband – he cooked more than I did, and he cleaned, ironed and did the shopping.

I had moved to another job, while Rod was still with our old company. His work involved a certain amount of travelling but we were both used to that and I trusted him completely.

When I discovered that I was pregnant with Jamie I was so happy. I did the test on my own at home and I couldn't wait to tell Rod when he got home that night. When he walked in and I broke the news he was thrilled too, and opened a bottle of champagne. If I saw a flicker of doubt cross his face, I ignored it, too thrilled not to believe that he didn't feel exactly the same as I did.

But as my pregnancy progressed things began to change between us. Rod became more distant, he worked later and travelled more often – always with plausible excuses – and even at home he spent more time apart from me. He suddenly decided to take up photography and would take off with his cameras, telling me that he'd be back in a few hours.

I was happy to be pregnant and was enjoying every stage of the process as the bump grew, but I began to feel very lonely. When I asked Rod if he had any doubts he said no, he was fine, and I couldn't get him to say anything more. But I got the feeling that he just didn't really want to be around me.

When Jamie was born Rod came with me to the hospital. But at the crucial moment he wasn't there – he'd gone off an hour earlier, saying that he needed some air. He came back when Jamie was a few minutes old and was delighted with his son, holding him for so long that I had to demand him back for a cuddle.

After that things improved a bit. Rod was around a lot more – in fact, he was a perfect hands-on dad. There was just one thing wrong: he didn't seem to fancy me any more. He hadn't wanted to make love when I was pregnant, saying that he didn't want to hurt the baby. And he didn't want to make love after Jamie was born. He made all kinds of excuses, but the bottom line was that he wouldn't come near me. I did everything I could to make myself attractive and organise time for us to spend alone – but nothing worked.

I hoped that things would change with time, and to a small extent they did. About a year after Jamie's birth we began to make love occasionally and I realised that I would have to settle for that. I had a good husband – I believed – a gorgeous son and no real problems.

We carried on like that until Josh was conceived. I

had wanted a second child for a couple of years, so I was thrilled to bits to find that I was pregnant again. But this time there was no disguising the doubt on Rod's face when I told him. He went very quiet, and when I asked 'Aren't you pleased?' I could see that it was an effort for him to say 'Of course.'

I was puzzled and disappointed by his reaction, but I couldn't get to the bottom of it. Didn't he want another child? I asked. Was something wrong? But Rod couldn't – or wouldn't – give me a real answer. He was vague and just said that of course he was happy, he just had a lot of work issues on his mind.

The early stages of my pregnancy were fine. But as time went on I began to feel very tired and unwell. At thirty weeks I went for a check-up and was told that the baby wasn't thriving – he wasn't growing as he should. I was terrified and the next few weeks were very hard to go through. Rod was upset too, but he was being so distant that we couldn't really share our fears.

At thirty-six weeks they decided to induce the birth. I was so relieved when, after a difficult labour, Josh was born. He was whisked straight off to an incubator and we were told that he was a little small and, more importantly, he had breathing difficulties and a chest infection.

After a very worrying couple of days, and many tests, I was given the unbelievable news that both Josh and I were HIV-positive. They sent a counsellor to tell me, and I just stared at her, aghast. 'I can't be, we can't be,' I kept saying. 'Where could I have got it? I haven't been with another man for eight years.'

The counsellor tried to get me to calm down, but I was in tears and close to hysteria. This couldn't be true – they must have made a mistake, I insisted. At that stage I just didn't even think of Rod: I felt that I alone must be in some way to blame. I kept asking if I could have caught the virus through some means other than unprotected sex. 'It's possible,' the counsellor told me, 'but unlikely.'

Eventually she left me and I lay in my hospital bed feeling that my world had just shattered. And it was then, as I lay thinking about what she'd said, that I understood – it was Rod, it had to be. He must have had an affair. Not only did I face the distress due to the life-threatening infection that my son and I now carried, but the double heartbreak of knowing that my husband must have been unfaithful, and must also be carrying the virus. What had Rod done? Was it a one-off? I asked myself. A one-night stand, a prostitute? I thought of how reluctant he had been to have sex with me and how at the time I couldn't understand it.

When he came in to visit me that afternoon I could barely look at him. I didn't want to discuss it in the public ward, but it was news that couldn't wait. Josh was already beginning treatment and I'd been told that he would have to stay in hospital for days and perhaps weeks.

Rod's face went white when I told him that Josh and I both had HIV. 'I haven't been with anyone else,' I said. 'So it has to be you. Please tell me the truth – don't make things worse by lying.'

Rod told me he'd had a brief affair on a work trip and that he bitterly regretted it. 'She <u>was nothing</u>,' he kept saying. 'It was just two nights and I <u>never</u> saw her again.' For some reason I felt that he was lying, but he insisted it was the truth so I tried to accept it.

Rod said that he had no idea he had the virus. He was tested immediately and of course the result was positive. He said how sorry he was, but I didn't want to hear it. He had given our baby what might be a death sentence, all because of a thoughtless moment of pleasure.

I asked Rod to move out, but he begged me to give it another go. And because Josh was sick and we would have so much to face, being treated ourselves while looking after him and Jamie, I eventually agreed that Rod could stay. 'One more chance,' I told him. 'Don't let me down again.'

The next few weeks were tough. Josh was very sick, but eventually he recovered and we were able to take him home. We tried to come to terms with what had happened and rebuild our family life, but I found that my heart just wasn't in it.

I thought things were as bad as they could get, but there was another bombshell waiting to drop. I still found it hard to trust Rod so I searched his clothing every day for evidence of an affair, terrified that he might still be seeing this other woman. When Josh was six months old I did come across a letter to Rod in his jeans pocket. It was a love letter, all right – but it was from a man. It was signed by someone called Kyle.

Once again I was bewildered. What on earth did it mean? You'll think me thick, but I felt that I couldn't take in any more shocks. An affair with a woman was bad enough – but a man? When Rod came home I put the letter in front of him. Perhaps he had wanted me to find it, because this time there was no story, no bluster or denial. He admitted that he had been having a gay affair – and that it wasn't the first. There had been several – lots, in fact, he said. He had always wondered if he was gay, and when I was pregnant he'd realised that he no longer fancied me and it was men he wanted.

The final admission, and the death knell for our marriage, was when he told me that he had known he had HIV. He had even been to a special counselling centre about it: he'd been seeing someone, talking to them about the gay affairs and the mess he'd got his life into. But, despite this, he'd had unprotected sex with me and given me the virus. When I asked him why he hadn't at least protected me he was almost casual. 'I could hardly suddenly start using condoms, could I?' he said. 'You wanted another baby. I just hoped you wouldn't get it.'

I was so furious and hurt that it was all I could do

not to punch him. Instead I went upstairs, put his clothes into a bin bag and threw them out of the front door. He begged me to at least talk, but I was past talking. I threw him out after his clothes and the next morning I had the locks changed.

My own husband had done something so unimaginably cruel that for days I just couldn't take it in. He had knowingly endangered my life and that of our new son. He had carried on sleeping with me while going out and having sex with men – lots of men. And when he knew that he had the virus his cowardice had stopped him from telling me the truth.

Rod wasn't a wife-beater or a violent man. But I reckon what he did to Josh and me was worse than battering. At least if I'd been battered my scars would fade and I could make a new start. But with HIV – well, it won't fade. I will have to take medication for the rest of my life, and I don't know how long the rest of my life will be.

My priority now is the boys and caring for them. I do everything I can to give them a good life. I try to look after all of us well, eating healthy food and getting enough rest. That includes me because I need to be around for them.

I have had lots of support – I joined a great organisation for women with HIV and meeting other women in the same situation has really helped. I've also seen a special HIV counsellor who's given me comfort and advice. I've got people I can talk to, I keep up with the latest medical developments and I do everything I can to stay well. I do my best to stay optimistic but every now and then I can't help shedding a few tears at the thought of either losing Josh or dying myself and having to leave the boys. I've written them letters, telling them how much I love them, and I've put them, with a box of photos and mementoes, in a safe place for them to have if anything happens to me. I've asked my sister to be their guardian if the worst happens, and I know she'll do a good job. But I want to be there for them myself – more than anything on earth I want that.

There were tears in the eyes of both of us by the time Linda had finished. I felt so touched by her bravery and the way she was coping. Her husband might have been in denial but Linda definitely wasn't. She had faced the worst that might happen and had prepared for it, and perhaps that was why she was able, despite the burden she carried, to be so full of life.

15
Brian

When it comes to the abuse of children, I believe we all have a duty to look out for the signs and report any worries or concerns that we have. We all get nervous about interfering in other people's families but there are times when interfering is the right thing to do. This was never more true than in the case of my friend Gwen, who reported the case of a child who she felt needed help. Gwen was ignored and accused of being a busybody, but she refused to be sidelined and kept on and on trying until the child, a little boy called Brian, was helped.

I first came across Brian – and Gwen, the brave woman who stood up for him – through the special-needs nursery where my son LJ had been given a place. It had been a long, hard struggle for us to find help for LJ, ever since his problems began after his MMR vaccination.

When I was told that he had learning difficulties I was devastated. It was a crushing blow for me and for LJ's dad, my first husband John McCutcheon, to learn that our beautiful blonde angel would need help throughout his educational life.

Only another parent of a special-needs child can understand how hard it is to be told that your child is different to other kids. You feel a strange mixture of grief, protectiveness and determination – grief for what the child will miss out on, protectiveness because having special needs makes them more vulnerable, and determination to do the very best you can for them, no matter what it takes.

LJ was born six weeks early, by emergency Caesarean, in June 1991, after he had stopped moving in the womb. He weighed just under six pounds – and was kept in special care for twelve days. It was a worrying time, but to our delight he thrived and put on weight. His traumatic birth had left no ill effects and LJ came home a normal, healthy baby. As he became a toddler we realised that he was very bright – by eighteen months he had a much bigger than average vocabulary and was like a little parrot, able to repeat with amazing accuracy words and phrases he heard.

Martine was fifteen when LJ was born, but she adored him and always went straight to cuddle him and play with him when she came home from school or work. We all doted on him, our chubby, happy little boy with his mass of blond curls, his bright blue eyes and his heart-melting smile.

When the time came for his routine MMR – measles, mumps and rubella vaccination – I thought nothing of it. The vaccination was relatively new – it hadn't been around when Martine was small – but it sounded like a good idea. When I took LJ in for his jab the doctor commented on how well he was speaking. I rolled up LJ's sleeve and when the needle went in he made no move, but afterwards his little lip wobbled and he said 'Hurt, Mummy.'

I cuddled him and then we set off home and LJ fell asleep on the way. At home I laid him on the sofa and soon afterwards I noticed that he was hot and restless. Within a short time he had developed a very high temperature. Worried, I tried to rouse him, but he wouldn't wake. When eventually he opened his eyes only the whites showed and he began to choke. Terrified, I realised that he was fitting because his temperature was so high. I scooped him up and rushed upstairs to put him in a cool bath.

I called John, who raced home. We rang for a doctor, but as we waited LJ had several more fits. Afraid to wait any longer, we wrapped him in wet towels and drove him to hospital. As I walked in, holding his limp body, a nurse took him from me and I broke down and sobbed.

A doctor saw LJ straight away. He was given medication to control the fits and transferred to the children's ward, where blood tests revealed that he had the rubella virus. A few days earlier I'd met a woman at the mother-and-toddler group whose daughter had just had rubella – LJ must have caught it from her. He'd had no symptoms but the doctors explained that, with his immune system already trying to cope with rubella, the vaccination had overloaded it.

When we took LJ home from hospital a week later it was painfully clear that he had changed dramatically. The bright, sunny little boy who had always been curious about everything around him was gone.

It was as though the clock had been turned back and LJ had lost most of what he had learned. He didn't speak and took little interest in anything. He found it hard to feed himself or grab hold of an object, his walking was unsteady, he was clumsy and bumped into things and he cried continuously.

Worst of all, his fits continued, day and night. We had to take turns watching him, never knowing when he would have a fit. Very soon both John and I were exhausted, as well as sick with worry. We took LJ to every specialist we could find, trying to get a diagnosis and some help for him, but no one was able to give us any answers.

I hoped against hope that he would recover and become the chatty little boy that he had once been. But as month after month passed with no improvement it was hard not to despair. A speech therapist we took him to told us that she believed he would never speak. It was devastating news. Would the words he spoke after the injection – 'Hurt, Mummy' – be his last-ever words?

John and I refused to give up. We did everything we could to stimulate LJ and encourage him to talk –

playing games with him, reading to him and talking to him constantly – but nothing seemed to work and his progress in other areas, like walking and feeding, was very, very slow.

After many trips and appointments to see various specialists, LJ was assessed and given a statement of special needs by the local educational authority. It was decided that he should attend a special-needs nursery to help him with his learning needs and social development.

We wanted LJ to be with other children and had already looked into specialist nurseries for children with special needs. He was on the waiting list for one, close to our home, but a place hadn't become available and we decided that we couldn't wait any longer. To get LJ into a suitable nursery we moved house, to Harold Hill in Essex.

There was a lovely nursery there and we were delighted when LJ was given a place to start in September, a couple of months later. That summer was a turning point for him. In June he had his fifth birthday and not long afterwards, as I was getting him dressed one morning, he started to move his lips. Eventually, with an effort, he spoke. 'Try, Mummy, me try,' he said. I hugged him and ran to tell John and Martine. They were thrilled – neither of them had ever doubted that LJ would talk again one day.

By the time he started at his new nursery he could say a few words, and the nursery staff were wonderful, supporting the work we were doing with him at home and encouraging him in every way. LJ settled in really well and made friends with several of the other children.

The nursery was a truly special place with kind and caring teachers and assistants. It had an atmosphere of love and warmth and every child was given attention. The children were embraced and cared for with real feeling and all the staff were totally devoted to helping them. The children there had a wide variety of different needs and social development problems, so it was a challenge for the staff. But they coped with patience and humour.

I can remember one child who would scream and would also kick and bite the staff, but they managed to calm her with loving words and lots of cuddles. It was only after a few weeks that I realised that the little girl couldn't talk and the screaming fits were her only way of communicating.

The children were encouraged to learn through play. Sign language was used to help develop their communication skills and as the weeks passed I noticed a great difference in LJ and his fellow classmates. All except one, a little boy called Brian. Brian attended another unit, but the children shared play sessions, and although I didn't see him much, I noticed that he wasn't doing well.

Brian was tiny and skinny – in fact, he seemed to be no more than a bag of bones. He always looked as if he needed a good wash and a few square meals. He was a timid little boy who would get startled and hide in the corner if there was a sudden noise. He seemed frightened of his own shadow and I wondered what could have made him so easily scared.

At the end of the day, Brian would look brighter and happier than he had when he'd arrived at the nursery in the morning. After being washed and tidied, given a good meal and hearing the tender and encouraging words of the staff he looked so much better. But it never lasted. The next morning he would be pushed through the door by his mother, looking dishevelled, dirty and terrified all over again. I was baffled by this, and wondered what his problems were and what was happening to him at home.

During LJ's time at the nursery I became very good friends with two of the other mums. Maggie had a son with autism and Gwen had a son who hadn't been diagnosed formally but had obvious problems. We would all meet up once a week for a coffee morning and talk about how our sons were getting on, sharing ideas and support. One particular morning Gwen mentioned Brian, who was friends with her son. I had felt touched by the sight of Brian, and was intrigued to learn more about the little boy. No one was quite sure what Brian's behavioural and developmental problems were, Gwen explained. But he was the youngest of six children from a troubled home.

His father, Reg, was a rather brutish man whose beliefs and traditions were old-fashioned and out-dated. He worked as a labourer on a building site all week, only to end up spending most of his hard-earned cash at the Four Feathers pub every Friday night. As Reg staggered home at the end of the evening his downtrodden wife Maureen would pre-pare herself for the beating that he would almost certainly mete out once he realised his dinner was dried up and inedible.

With little or no money, Maureen struggled to pay the bills and buy food for the children, all of whom were frightened of their father. When he was around, the older children managed to stay out of his way. But Brian, as the youngest and weakest, was an easy victim and the butt of his father's vile temper.

Prejudiced, ignorant and cruel, his father was so furious about Brian's problems that he refused to accept that Brian was even his son. Instead of helping the child, as most parents would, he blamed him for being different and punished him.

'He's no son of mine, skinny little bastard. He ain't right in the head,' he would curse, aiming a kick or a thump at Brian. Completely lacking the protective instinct that most parents have towards a small and fragile child, Reg was ashamed of his son. Boys ought to be robust and strong, he said, they ought to be fighters, and if they weren't, well, they were useless. Maureen hadn't been able to help her son either.

Afraid of her husband, crushed in spirit and with six children to look after, she had done nothing to protect Brian from his brutish father or his bullying older brothers.

Social services had been alerted and they visited the family. But the decision was taken not to break up the family unit by taking Brian away. Instead, they decided to offer help and support for the family by giving Brian a place at the special-needs nursery.

Each day Brian would be frogmarched up the corridor to the nursery unit. All the mothers would stare at Maureen as she dragged the little boy along, so quickly that his feet hardly touched the ground. She made no attempt to talk with any of the other mothers – in fact, she would scowl and give dirty looks as she passed. It was almost as if she felt degraded at being there and accepting that her child was different made her ashamed.

She would open the classroom door and, without even greeting the teaching staff, would shove Brian in as quickly as she could. She would lift her head, sniff loudly and mutter obscenities under her breath. She could often be heard saying 'bloody mongols', or 'idiot kids'. It was amazing to witness the ignorance of the woman and her hostile words were very hurtful to all the other parents, whose children she was insulting.

Each day that passed, Brian had a new bruise, cut or scratch. His hair was often matted and his clothes were always too big for him and dirty. Although the nursery staff did their very best to help Brian, he was unlikely to make any real progress as long as he had to be returned each evening to suffer abuse at the hands of his parents.

Beaten by his drunken father, bullied by his older brothers and sisters and virtually starved by his mother, Brian's life was torture, with his time at the nursery the only respite from the misery he suffered at home.

I was shocked to hear this appalling story. My heart ached for Brian. The abuse of a special-needs child must surely be the worst kind of abuse there is – such children are even more vulnerable and unable to speak up for themselves than others. I found it hard to believe that the authorities thought it best to leave Brian at home to continue suffering. Gwen agreed with me.

'I have contacted the authorities many times,' she said. 'Of course they never want to listen to me: they tell me the case is being dealt with and that my comments will be noted. It makes me livid because while they're spouting bureaucratic jargon a child is suffering. They don't realise how bad things are for him – they think the family is just poor and struggling, and they don't accept that the parents are actually harming Brian. But he shouldn't be left at home and I won't give up until he is taken into safety. I know the nursery staff are worried too – they send in reports on his condition. We all need to speak up for children like

Brian because they can't speak for themselves. I don't care if they do think I'm an interfering old cow, I'm not giving up.'

I agreed, and Maggie and I both offered to back Gwen's campaign to help Brian in any way we could. 'Thanks,' she said. 'We must all batter on the authorities' doors until they take notice. Of course sometimes it's best to leave a child with their family, if the family wants to change things for the better. But sometimes nothing's going to change and the child needs to be protected.'

A few weeks later I noticed that Brian was no longer visiting the nursery. When I asked Gwen what had happened she told me that he had at last been taken into care. She had gone round to see the head of social services and refused to leave until he reviewed Brian's case.

Sad as I was that Brian would grow up without his family, I couldn't help but feel enormous relief that he would no longer suffer cruelty and neglect. I told Gwen how right I thought she had been to speak out, and to encourage others to speak out too. Brian needed help, and Gwen was the one who'd been brave enough to make sure he got it.

The nursery staff were also very relieved that Brian had been taken to safety. They had done their best, but they could only love and protect him while he was actually in their care.

Gwen had become very fond of Brian and she followed his progress. A few months later we were chatting over coffee and I asked her how he was and whether, in his new home, they had been able to work out exactly was wrong with him.

'That's the amazing thing,' Gwen told me. 'It turned out that Brian wasn't a special-needs child at all. Once he was removed from the terrors of home he blossomed. The staff at his new nursery began to notice that although he was timid he was actually showing many signs of being bright and alert when reading, playing and interacting with the teachers. Tests by an educational psychologist proved what the staff suspected: that Brian had no learning difficulties. All his problems and his apparent special needs stemmed from the abuse and neglect he suffered at the hands of his parents which left him so traumatised that he was unable to function normally.'

Hearing this was both shocking and wonderful. I was so happy that Brian, who had suffered enough in his short life, did not, after all, have learning difficulties. But at the same time it was awful to realise that cruelty and neglect could have such a devastating effect on a child, so much so that everyone had been convinced that he really did have educational and functional problems.

It only proved how powerful a child's environment is in shaping who they are. Brian was clearly a sensitive and gentle child whose parents had no understanding of his needs and no concern for him. He wasn't a survivor like his more robust siblings – he was the smaller, needier child at the bottom of the pack and his parents despised him for it. Instead of helping him to cope they created more problems for him.

A year later I was delighted to hear from Gwen that Brian was happy with his foster parents and was thriving. Although he was still small for his age he was doing incredibly well at school and his teachers had great hopes for him. His confidence was growing, he was making friends and everyone hoped that, in time, the emotional scars left by his unhappy home life would fade, even if they never fully disappeared.

As for my own son, he continued to make steady progress and we were hopeful that he might eventually catch up with his age group and go into mainstream schooling.

It wasn't until LJ was six that we finally got a proper diagnosis of his problems. A specialist we took him to told me that he was both dyslexic and dyspraxic. The dyslexia meant that he would struggle with reading and writing and the dyspraxia caused him problems with coordination, making him clumsy and disorientated. He also had speech and language problems and would always need special-needs teaching.

Most devastatingly of all the specialist confirmed what I had always, in my heart, known to be true – that LJ had been damaged by the MMR inoculation. There was nothing we could do about it – like thousands of other parents we had no proof. But it was heartbreaking to think that a routine vaccination could have changed his life – and ours – so powerfully.

John and I continued to do everything we could to help LJ's progress, feeding him healthy food, buying him stimulating toys and taking him on outings, including many trips on his beloved trains.

Today LJ is a happy and healthy teenager who has exceeded all expectations and has made wonderful progress. He is also a sweet-natured, generous and much-loved son who has brought us immense joy.

And Brian? Strangely, I came across him again only a year or two ago. I got in touch with my old friend Gwen, keen to catch up on our mutual news, and she told me that she had seen Brian, who had remained friends with her son. At fifteen Brian was doing extremely well, taking his GCSEs and dreaming of becoming an engineer. He had remained with the same foster parents, who had adopted him, and he had an adopted younger brother he was very close to.

I was so glad to hear that Brian had not only survived the misery of his early years but had proved his ignorant parents wrong by turning out to be the kind of son anyone would be hugely proud of. And most of all I was proud of Gwen, for refusing to turn a blind eye and instead being the kind of person who would stand up and shout out loud on behalf of a child who needed her help.

16
Stephanie

Stephanie was a girl I was at school with – not one of my closest friends but someone I knew in passing. We met again a few years after leaving school, when both of us were young mothers, and that was when I heard her story.

Stephanie's is a story of betrayal by someone she had been led to believe would look after her. Stephanie had every reason to trust this man. Her parents knew him, he was friendly with her father, and when he and his wife asked Stephanie to babysit for their children her parents were happy to approve of the arrangement. Yet he took advantage of her in the most appalling way and as a result changed the course of her life.

I understand well what it's like to be led into a false sense of security by an adult who seems kind and trustworthy. When I was ten we lived in Monteagle Court, a block of flats not far from London's Hoxton Market. Nearby was a piece of waste ground where we children played, and next to that was a site on which had been a disused factory that we kids called the Secret F. We were heartbroken when the factory and the 'jungle' next to it were bulldozed to the ground.

A fence was erected round the site and a caretaker spent his days there, in a small wooden hut. He was kind and friendly to us kids. Dozens of us used to play on the waste ground and he'd let us onto the factory site through a hole in the fence and invite us into his hut for a chat while he brewed his tea on a small primus stove. We all liked to go and visit George, and for me and my sister Kim his little hut became a bit of a refuge from the horrors of home. One day, when I'd managed to escape from Dad's clutches, I was wandering around looking for somewhere to go. I didn't dare go home for the next few hours, knowing how furious Dad would be that I'd given him the slip when he wanted to have his evil way with me. It was freezing cold and I decided to visit George in his hut. I knew he'd offer me a seat and a cup of tea which would warm me up.

George was as welcoming as ever, giving me a friendly smile, inviting me to sit on the stool near the paraffin heater and handing me a mug of tea. But as we chatted I sensed something change and I began to feel anxious. George asked me whether I had a boyfriend, and began moving too close to me. The expression on his face reminded me of Dad's when he wanted to abuse me. And the next thing I knew George was putting his arm around me and trying to kiss me full on the mouth.

Horrified, I managed to push him off and run out of the hut, tears streaming down my cheeks. I couldn't believe that nice friendly old George had done such a thing. I wondered if all men were like that, waiting for a chance to take advantage. I knew I could never go to George's hut again and I felt I had lost a friend. I was so upset that when I went home I got the kitchen scissors and cut off my long blonde hair, trying to make myself ugly so that men like George and Dad would leave me alone.

George's betrayal of trust went deep with me. I never forgot the shock and hurt of realising that he wasn't a good person after all and that I had got him all wrong. So I understood very well what happened to Stephanie, and how she must have felt.

It's funny, but I can remember some parts of my time at school vividly and other parts just seem to escape me. I can remember names of teachers and some of my classmates even now, but when I bumped into Stephanie only a few years after leaving school I couldn't remember her name.

It was a rainy day and to kill a few hours before I had to go back to my dingy bed-and-breakfast halfway house I called into the Geffrye Museum for a cup of coffee. It was a small museum close to my old home, somewhere we had loved to go as children.

Martine was not yet two and I had her with me in the pushchair. Sitting opposite me was a girl the same age as me with her own young child – an adorable little boy with blond curls and big blue eyes who looked about three years old. As this girl and I started to talk about our babies, it dawned on both of us that we had been at school together.

Stephanie had been a studious girl, while I had been a bit of a tearaway. So when I left school at fifteen to start my first job at Marks and Spencer's she had opted to stay on. I'd always imagined that she'd do well in her exams and go on to have an exciting job. So I was surprised to find that, just like me, she was a single mum.

We laughed about her and her studies and all the trouble I got into at school. I offered to buy her another coffee and she agreed, and over the second cup we got talking about how we'd become mothers. I told her a little about Keith and the many mistakes I'd made, and said that now I had my daughter she was all that mattered. Although I was in a horrible damp and ugly halfway house, I was waiting for a council flat and was determined to make a good life for us.

After I'd told her my story, Stephanie went very quiet for a while. She was deep in thought and she looked at me long and hard before speaking. 'Charlie's dad is not on the scene any more, but for different reasons. You see, his dad raped me, and although I love my son I'll never be able to tell him what happened to his dad and why I never married him.'

I was still only twenty and I couldn't help looking shocked.

'It's OK, Jen, I haven't told many people but when I do they react in the same way,' she said. 'It's funny, but

I hadn't seen anyone from school in a long while until I met you. I suppose that when it happened I shut myself away. I was too ashamed to continue at school so I left and never did pass my A levels, though I'd got some good grades at GCSE. I had dreams of going to college – I wanted to work in law. I've got as close to it as I can – I work part-time in a local solicitor's office as a litigation secretary. It's OK, but not quite what I imagined for myself.'

I asked Stephanie if she would tell me what had happened, and she nodded. What follows is her story.

When I was sixteen I had a local babysitting job a couple of evenings a week which earned me a bit of cash. The family were old friends of my dad's and it all worked out well. The kids weren't too bad and after they'd gone to bed I could do my homework. And the money meant that I could save up for a few of the things I wanted.

I never imagined anything would happen to me at George and Ann's house. After all, I'd been going there for a few months and everything had always been fine. The kids – Davey and Susie – were nice and I'd play with them for a bit before putting them to bed.

Ann was always good to me, leaving me out something to eat and asking about how my schoolwork was going. And George – a big overweight bloke with grey hair – was friendly enough.

On the night everything changed they had gone to

the pub for their usual Friday night out. I almost always babysat for them on Friday nights and I didn't expect them back before closing time, so I was surprised to hear the door open at about ten-thirty.

As soon as they walked in it was obvious that Ann had had far too many drinks. She was staggering about and falling all over the place. It was also obvious that they'd been arguing – the atmosphere between them was terrible. I hoped that I could slip out quickly, but all of a sudden they started arguing again and Ann began screaming abuse at George, telling him that she'd had enough of him leering at young girls and that he was a nonce!

I cringed in embarrassment, wishing that I didn't have to hear them fighting. George was furious, and dragged Ann upstairs, presumably to the bedroom. A few minutes later he reappeared and apologised for her behaviour. He offered to drive me home and although I said it was OK and that I'd walk, he insisted. He'd clearly had a couple of drinks himself and I hated the idea of getting in the car with him, not because he might be over the drink limit, which people didn't think about so much then, but because I was embarrassed about the row they'd had. I just wanted to get away, but he was insistent, saying it was the least he could do, and I felt I had to say yes.

If only I hadn't. I've thought a thousand times since that I could have insisted on walking. Instead I was polite, and it cost me so much.

In the car, George started to talk about Ann's outburst and apologised again. But then he said something that made the hair on the back of my neck stand on end. 'I think she's guessed that I fancy you,' he murmured in a suggestive tone. I wasn't sure what to say. This was my dad's mate and he was hitting on me. He was fifty and I was seventeen and I just couldn't believe it. It had never even occurred to me that a man like that might fancy me – or, worse, try it on. I thought that he had to be having a laugh, and I told him in no uncertain terms that he definitely was not my type.

By this time he had drawn up near my house and I was about to get out. But George was too quick for me. He grabbed me and his mouth was over mine in seconds. He forced his tongue into my mouth – I could taste the whisky on his breath and wanted to gag. I was struggling but I had no chance against him, he was so strong. It sounds strange, but I felt that all my strength had deserted me and before I could struggle any more he had got me pinned on the seat, undone his trousers, pulled my skirt up and my knickers down and forced himself inside me. He kept saying how lovely I was as he continued to push himself into me and squeeze my breasts so hard that I could almost feel them bruising.

It was all over very quickly, thank God. As soon as George was off me he did his trousers up and quite casually told me to sort myself out and get myself indoors. In a complete daze, I obeyed him as if I was a small child. I walked to my front door feeling as though I was in a trance. I could hardly believe it had happened. I turned round just as he drove off. He didn't even look back at me.

I walked into my house and made my way upstairs. I recall Mum shouting out from the front room and asking me if everything was OK and I answered yes.

In my room I undressed and then went to the bathroom to take a bath. All I wanted to do was to scrub every trace of George off me. I washed for hours and cleaned my teeth three times. I really don't know what I was thinking: looking back it all seems like a blur. I had no idea what I was going to do – I couldn't even think about it.

In the end what I did was – nothing. I was too shocked, too afraid, too ashamed. I just pushed it all to the back of my mind and carried on as if nothing had happened.

A few things did change – I never babysat for anyone again, including George and Ann. When they asked me, the next week, I said I had too much schoolwork and wouldn't be able to come again. Mum asked me if everything was all right: she knew how much the money had meant to me, but I assured her that I was fine and just didn't fancy babysitting any more.

Why did I decide not to tell anyone? I've thought a lot about that. I think I just felt so ashamed, as though it was my fault and I should have seen it coming and been able to stop George. I kept thinking that if only I'd walked home it would never have happened. And there was another reason – I was afraid that if I accused George he would deny it or, worse, say that I had given him the come-on. I convinced myself that no one would believe me, especially my dad. After all, he and George had been friends for years.

All I wanted was to put it all behind me, as though it had never happened. But I didn't realise at the time that that was never going to be possible. When I missed my next period it honestly didn't occur to me that I might be pregnant. I just thought it was what happened sometimes. But when I missed my second and third periods it dawned on me that I was going to have a baby – George's baby.

It wasn't until I was four months gone that I found the courage to tell my mum. She was shocked, but she was also understanding and asked me what I wanted to do. We went to the doctor together and he confirmed it. By then I was nineteen weeks pregnant and it was getting very late for an abortion. I thought over what to do for a couple of days, but in the end I knew I couldn't get rid of it. I could feel it kicking and that made it seem like a little person. And, after all, what had happened wasn't the baby's fault.

Dad had to be told and he made a big fuss, demanding to know who the father was. He and Mum knew I'd had a boyfriend a few months earlier and they thought it was him. I knew it wasn't – we'd split quite a while before George raped me. I told them it wasn't my ex, but I refused to say who it was and in the end I think they assumed it was a one-night stand. I got a lot of lectures from Dad about morals. It hurt, because apart from my ex-boyfriend, who I'd been with for two years, I'd never had sex with anyone else until that horrible night with George. I just wasn't a one-night stand kind of girl, but without telling my parents the truth what could I say to defend myself? And somehow I just *couldn't* tell them the truth. I suppose I felt that in some way I must have been to blame. And I was terrified that I wouldn't be believed.

I have tried several times to tell them, but I still can't. I'm not sure why: it just feels such a big issue, I suppose. The longer I leave it the harder it is to come out with it. I did tell a social worker who helped me after Charlie was born, and a health visitor. They were both lovely. But I can't face telling my parents.

They've been good to me. After the initial fuss they both stood by me. Mum went to all my antenatal appointments with me and was there at the birth. And despite the way he was conceived, I loved Charlie from the moment he came into the world. He looked at me with those big blue eyes and I just thought – he's nothing to do with George, he's mine.

I lived at home for Charlie's first few months. I had left school when I was pregnant, I just couldn't face carrying on and all the questions I'd be asked by the other girls. After Charlie was born I was a full-time mum for a year. By then the social worker had helped me to get my own little flat and I got a job with a local solicitor's office as a clerk.

Mum looked after Charlie while I was at work and I loved my job and soon got promoted to a secretarial job in the litigation department. I've made a good life and I plan to go on and study law later, if I can find a way.

As for George, I've only seen him once since that dreadful night. When I was pregnant Dad, Mum and I were in a local pub and George and Ann came in. Do you know, he just sat down and chatted away to my dad and didn't even look at me. But Ann was silent. She gazed at me as if I had committed a murder and I was sure she knew – or had guessed – the truth.

An hour had passed and the rain had cleared by the time Stephanie had finished her tale. She got to her feet, putting Charlie back into his buggy and strapping him in.

'Don't feel sorry for me, Jen, I don't need it,' she said. 'I'm OK and I'm not sorry I've got Charlie. Well, I must be off. It's been great to see you again and I wish you lots of luck.'

I was a little taken aback at the speed with which Stephanie rushed off. Perhaps she felt a bit embarrassed after telling me the whole story. I've found this on other occasions – sometimes it's as if when someone tells you something very painful and personal that's all they can cope with and they need to end the conversation quickly.

I thought a lot about Stephanie's story and wished her well. I never expected to see her again but funnily enough I did, about five years later. I was on my way to catch a train at Liverpool Street station – I was by then working in a temporary recruitment agency in the City – when I passed a very smart young woman who was wearing a black suit and holding a briefcase and lots of files. I recognised Stephanie immediately and said hello.

She seemed bemused. 'Do I know you?' she asked. When I prompted her memory, she looked a little uncomfortable and said, 'Oh yes, sorry, Jenny, I was miles away.' I asked her how she was and she told me that she was now training to be a lawyer. I was delighted for her and asked after Charlie. 'He's fine,' she said. 'He's doing well at school.'

After this brief exchange Stephanie excused herself, explaining that she had to meet someone and couldn't stop. She hurried off and I went to catch my train.

For a while afterwards I thought about our chance meeting and wondered why Stephanie had seemed so distant. Perhaps it was because she had moved on and had left a lot of the past behind her – and that included our conversation that rainy day.

Despite her initial rebuff I was pleased for her. She had clearly made a success of her life. What could have been a tragedy and stopped her ever achieving her ambition had, because of her determination, been no more than a diversion. Stephanie had gone on to achieve her ambition of becoming a lawyer, and I hoped she felt very proud of herself.

If Stephanie wanted to forget the past – and me with it – I had no objections. Everyone has different ways of dealing with things and for some people that means leaving the past behind.

And who are we to judge? My sister Kim kept our years of abuse very quiet and only spoke out very recently. She has said that, despite everything, she had still felt guilty and ashamed for many years and maybe this applied to Stephanie too. Some of us are able to talk about the past and move on with our lives in that way, whilst some of us cope by keeping it locked away. And I've learned over the years that whatever works for each one of us is fine, because in the end we are all fellow survivors and that's what's really important.

Stephanie, like me, like every other person whose story has been told in this book, found the courage to go on with her life, to move forward and to make every moment count. Not one of them had given in, given up or settled for self-pity. That's why not one of them is a victim. In fact, quite the opposite: I think of them as quiet heroes, some of the most special people I have been lucky enough to meet.

Final Word

Each individual whose story has been told in this book has shown such courage and so much determination that I feel privileged to have met them.

Sometimes I have to stop and think about what goes on in our society and how many people have suffered and are still suffering. Each one of them needs to find their own hope, help and strength, and I'd like to believe that in some way, by telling my own story and those of the brave people in this book, I have helped them.

As a little girl, left to fend off my father's brutality and sexual advances, I felt alone, unloved and uncared for. Strength of will told me not to give up and that one day his reign of terror would come to an end and I would be free. I won't say it has been easy to forget those dark days; the memories of what happened to me as a child will always be there. But there is light at the end of the tunnel and writing my childhood memoirs down in my first book, *Behind Closed Doors*, certainly helped in the rebuilding of my life.

Like most abused children I became an abused adult as well. I grew up with such low self-esteem that I went from suffering abuse at the hands of my father to suffering once again at the hands of my daughter's father. My second book, *Silent Sisters*, covers my adult life and I hope it may have helped anyone dealing with domestic-abuse issues to realise that they needn't suffer alone – because help is out there!

I hope that my writing about the individuals in this book will help others who have demons that they need to conquer. Ultimately, of course, each person must find their own way through such troubled episodes of their lives. But whether they write, seek professional help, or simply rely on their own inner strength to combat what they have experienced, all those who have suffered abuse deserve recognition for their courage.

Finally, I would like to thank everyone involved with this book. All the wonderful friends and acquaintances who shared their experiences with me need to know what heroes they are, and how much I hope their stories will help others. I thank them all from the bottom of my heart. If you have suffered abuse and need help, remember that it is out there! Don't suffer in silence. If I can begin life the way I did and get through and come out at the end with a wonderful loving family, then so can you. Don't be afraid to live and be loved. Be a Victor and not a Victim for you are Not Alone!